Questions

God

Asks

Israel Wayne

My friend Israel Wayne has a rare combination of eloquence and practical wisdom. You will be encouraged, challenged, and blessed by this innovative book.

Michael Farris, author, founder of
Patrick Henry College and HSLDA

I want to thank Israel Wayne for writing this book, *Questions God Asks*. I found this book to be challenging and encouraging. Through the questions in this book, you will have a better understanding of the faithfulness of our Lord. It speaks as to how God challenged people all through Scripture. These questions still relate to us today in our own lives. This book will bless you and will help you grow in your spiritual walk with God.

Buddy Davis, artist, musician, speaker
with Answers in Genesis

Questions God Asks is truly insightful, enjoyable, and challenging. I know of no other book that takes such a unique approach to these vital, yet often overlooked questions. A must-read!

David Ravenhill, author and Bible teacher

Israel Wayne is a fresh young voice for a timeless biblical message. This book turns the table from the questions we often ask God to the key questions of the heart that God is continually asking us. Answering them could change your life.

Byron Paulus, Executive Director
Life Action Ministries

In a day when we often hear that our questions are autonomous on the mere condition that we have them, Israel Wayne reminds us that the God who made us has some questions for us. Ours are asked in our ignorance and, at times, our rebellion. His are asked as one who ultimately knows. He knows all. He knows us. There's much to learn on a journey that starts with God's questions, and Israel is a terrific guide.

John Stonestreet, speaker, the Chuck
Colson Center for Christian Worldview and
senior content advisor for Summit Ministries

Questions God Asks is a book that will be most helpful to Christians in understanding that when God asks questions, they are meant for our edification. In this book, Israel Wayne has demonstrated that our knowledge of all things in this life is tied directly to the God of truth who has revealed Himself and His truth to us in the Holy Scripture. Each question is meant to challenge the reader to consider how we are to obey and honor our God in all that He has commanded us. That as Christians we might better understand our purpose in our salvation and the life that He has ordered for us. This is a book which is a must-read for parents and children. It is a book that will stimulate you to think and teach you to think biblically.

Dr. Kenneth Talbot, President
Whitefield College and Theological Seminary

First printing: February 2014

New Leaf Press, P.O. Box 726, Green Forest, AR 72638

New Leaf Press is a division of the New Leaf Publishing Group, Inc.

ISBN: 978-0-89221-721-2
Library of Congress Number: 2013957738

Cover by Left Coast Design, Portland, Oregon

Unless otherwise noted, Scripture quotations are from the NASB version of the Bible.

Please consider requesting that a copy of this volume be purchased by your local library system.

Printed in the United States of America

Please visit our website for other great titles:
www.newleafpress.net

For information regarding author interviews, please contact the publicity department at (870) 438-5288.

New Leaf Press
A Division of New Leaf Publishing Group
www.newleafpress.net

Table of Contents

Introduction

In the innermost chambers of the celestial temple dwells the awesome presence of the only true and living God. Seraphim worship saying, "Holy, holy, holy is the LORD of hosts, the whole earth is full of His glory" (Isa. 6:3). The thresholds shake, and the Temple in which God resides is filled with smoke. On a throne, high and exalted, sits the Creator and Sustainer of the universe, the being whose breath spoke galaxies into existence. Unfathomable beauty, unapproachable light, unimaginable power, and untold wisdom belong to Him.

What kind of thoughts does a God like this think? What are His feelings? What occupies His mind? First John 3:20 informs us that God knows all things. Could a God who knows everything, who gives mankind his breath, have questions? As outlandish as it may seem to us, the Bible is filled with questions that God asks.

We ask questions when we don't understand a matter. God asks questions *because* He knows all matters infinitely. "Oh, the depth of the riches both of the wisdom and knowledge of God! How unsearchable are His judgments, and unfathomable His ways!" (Rom. 11:33).

That fact alone causes us to ask more questions. There is a vast difference between us and our Creator. We are so finite, but He is so infinitely infinite. We are so foolish, but He, in His very nature, is wisdom. We don't understand

God very well. We don't even understand ourselves. God, in contrast, knows the very secrets of our hearts (Ps. 44:21). That means He knows more about who we are than we are capable of knowing. Desires and motives in our hearts, which are hidden to our view, are exposed before His piercing gaze. That is why God asks questions. It couldn't possibly be for His benefit. His probing inquiries must certainly be to assist us. "The LORD searches all hearts, and understands every intent of the thoughts" (1 Chron. 28:9).

God doesn't throw inquiries to the wind; He aims them squarely at us. We are the target on which His interrogatory darts stick. As we examine the questions God asks, we will come to better understand our Maker — and ourselves as well. We will have to scrutinize our fundamental assumptions about God, human nature, relationships, origins, purpose, and destiny. The Judge of the universe has called us into account. We are required to explain to God things that seem beyond our understanding. The purpose isn't to condemn us, or to expose what truly miserable and wretched little imps we are. God, as a loving Father, probes our hearts and minds, plumbing the very depths of our souls to bring us into integrity (a cohesiveness and coherence) in our inmost being. May we brace ourselves for this holy cross-examination with an open and honest heart, knowing that it is for His glory and our good. It is time to stop demanding answers from God and begin answering the questions He asks of us.

Chapter 1

Where Were You?

(Origins — Job)

"Where were you when I laid the foundation of the earth? Tell Me, if you have understanding."

— Job 38:4

S ir, would you care for something to drink?"

"Sure, I'll take an apple juice."

I guess there is no point in trying to sleep. Have you ever tried to rest inside a hollow, metal cylinder, 35,000 feet above ground, in a seat that leans slightly forward, and you can't recline because the pilot hasn't turned off the seat-belt sign yet?

I was returning from Boise to Chicago, the final leg of a week-long speaking tour. As is often the case on these trips, I was exhausted. My sister, Mercy, was with me, sitting next to a man in his 60s who was looking out the window. Mercy and I have different approaches when it comes to airplane evangelism. Her goal is to have all of the passengers on the flight on their knees repenting of their sins before we land. I'll have to admit that when I am worn out from a long trip and don't feel like talking, I suddenly become a hyper-Calvinist!

God will save those He wills, I tell myself. *If they were meant to be saved they will be, if not, who am I to try to change them?* In the previous two flights, Mercy had managed to have extensive counseling sessions with two ladies who were intrigued with her faith. It didn't take long before she had attempted to engage the man beside her in dialogue.

"I disassemble and repair telescopes," he informed her. "Mostly I work on really old observatory telescopes from the 1800s." Suddenly my ears perked up.

"Do you study astronomy yourself?" I asked, leaning over my sister to introduce myself.

"Why yes, I do." The man replied. "I absolutely love it."

We chatted for a while about his fascinating occupation, and then I began to question him about his beliefs. "When you study astronomy," I began, "You can only do so because of the predictability of the orbits of the planets and the precision with which the universe operates, is that right?"

"That is true."

"When you think about the complexity of life and the precision of math and physics, what is your explanation for how it all came to be?"

"Oh, I have studied that in great detail. *National Geographic* and *Nova* have produced some excellent video documentaries that explain how everything began with a cosmic big bang, and from there, organic life (which has always existed) evolved from simple organisms to more complex ones, until eventually it became life as we know it today."

"So we are all just accidents?"

"Yes. Quite true. It is amazing to realize, but there is no other explanation."

From my questioning I believe he suspected that I held to a theistic worldview. I was trying out Aquinas' Cosmological Argument, which reasons that if something is designed, it must have a designer.

"Then why do we feel like our lives have meaning?" I inquired.

"Well, that is the deception of it all. In the end, we just die and that is all there is."

"Do you mean to tell me that we are sitting inside a hollow metal cylinder, flying hundreds of miles an hour, looking down upon the Rocky Mountains, expecting to arrive at an exact point of destination within five minutes of anticipated schedule, using physics and mathematics to compensate for all of the wind patterns and jet streams, and you have the mental capability to think about life's purpose and verbalize that we are nothing more than a cosmic accident, and not the result of intelligent design?"

"Yes, yes," he answered. "It is almost a miracle really, but that is how it is."

"It takes an amazing amount of faith to believe that!" I told him.

As our conversation "evolved," it became clear to me that this man, although quite intelligent, had chosen to adopt a worldview that fit his comfort level. He would much prefer to believe that his life was meaningless than to admit that there was a God to whom he was accountable. He told me that he has a Southern Baptist friend who gives him books on intelligent design and creation to read. He remains unconvinced. The reason he won't believe has nothing to do with the evidence. In spite of all evidence to the contrary, he religiously adheres to naturalism.

At one point I asked him, "Were you there at the beginning of time? Did you see the beginnings of the universe?" He conceded that he had not. "Then," I reminded him, "your belief is based on a philosophical presupposition or assumption, not on science, since you did not observe the origin of life." He wisely admitted this was true. "So," I continued, "we are both beginning on the same level.

Neither of us was there (when the universe began), so we both start with a model (creation or evolution), and we determine if the scientific evidence fits our belief system." He agreed once again.

"The question then, is not whether we believe in faith or in science; the fact is that we both begin outside of science and can only use science for evidence, not for proof."

These arguments are not new. They go back to the beginning of time.

As humans we desire to know why we are here and to make sense of the universe around us. This is Aquinas' argument from meaning. Somehow, we intuitively understand that it is important what happens to us. Even the most radical Darwinist grieves at the death of their child, or rejection by someone they love. They don't say, "Nothing more has happened than the decay of organic matter," or "This is merely one natural force repelling from another as they collide in space and time." No, they realize, instinctively, that life is significant.

The fact is, while we were not present when God spoke our world into existence, *He* was. The right question is not, "Does God exist?" The real question is, "Where were *you*?" When God laid out the heavens and fashioned the earth, He didn't need our permission, and He wasn't bound by our skepticism. The answer is that you existed in the mind of God thousands of years before you were born. When God fashioned creation, He did it with you in mind. Even if we are not mindful of God, He is mindful of us.

Your eyes have seen my unformed substance; and in Your book were all written the days that were ordained for me, when as yet there was not one of them (Ps. 139:16).

This planet called earth is uniquely fashioned to be able to sustain life. Your body is remarkably formed to allow you to live, move, and breathe (Acts 17:28). We will never understand all of the mysteries of creation (Eccles. 3:11).

"It is the glory of God to conceal a matter" (Prov. 25:2). But knowing that it is also the glory of kings to search out the hidden, we know that if we humble ourselves under God's mighty hand, He will teach us what we need to know. As with Job, we can't always comprehend or explain how or why God has worked in time and space, but we can say with him, "As for me, I know that my Redeemer lives, And at the last He will take His stand on the earth. Even after my skin is destroyed, Yet from my flesh I shall see God; Whom I myself shall behold, And whom my eyes will see and not another. My heart faints within me!" (Job 19:25–27).

I don't know all there is to know about God, but I do know Him. I can't know truth comprehensively, but I can know truth truly. I know that He made me, He sustains my life, He has a purpose for me, and I will live with Him eternally. I know that *He* knows all things because He is from the beginning. I know Him, and that is what I really need to know.

Chapter 2

Where Are You?

(Omnipresence — Adam and Eve)

Then the LORD God called to the man [Adam], and said to him, "Where are you?"

— Genesis 3:9

When I was about seven years old, I had a brilliant plan. I had finally discovered the ultimate hiding place. After careful consideration and deliberation, I waited for a busy summer Saturday when everyone in the family was engrossed in weekend chores. At just the right moment, I dashed downstairs, grabbed the car keys off the counter, and raced out the front door. Looking both ways to make sure the coast was clear, I ran to our Chevy sedan and fumbled to find the trunk key.

My heart was beating, my palms were sweating, and I could barely contain the nervous anticipation of implementing my scheme. At last, the correct key turned the lock and the trunk popped open. As quick as a flash, I removed the keys, put them in my pocket, jumped into the trunk, and pulled it down hard until it latched.

It was dark and silent. The only sound was a lawnmower running in our backyard. "What a great hiding place!" I declared softly to myself. "No one will *ever* find me in here!" No sooner had I uttered those fateful words than the ramifications of such a scenario crashed upon me like a tsunami on a peaceful beach. Suddenly, I began to panic. My heart was beating, my palms were sweating, and I could barely contain my fear as I dreaded what awaited me. *How long does it take for a body to decompose?* I thought to myself. *Oh yeah, that's right, you have to die first. How long does it take to die of starvation? No, wait, you die of thirst before you die from lack of food.*

It was getting quite warm. "How long does it take before you run out of oxygen?" I remembered a story I had heard of a boy who took short breaths in a somewhat similar situation to conserve air. I decided that I could either conserve air, or scream like crazy for someone to help me. I chose the latter. I don't know how long it took before I was rescued. Perhaps 5 minutes. Maybe 15. Whatever it was, it felt like an eternity. While I'm sure many busy mothers of young children would disagree, it can be a frightful thing to be left completely *alone*!

God's Omnipresence

> Where can I go from Your Spirit? Or where can I flee from Your presence? If I ascend to heaven, You are there; if I make my bed in Sheol [the grave], behold, You are there. If I take the wings of the dawn, if I dwell in the remotest part of the sea, even there Your hand will lead me, and Your right hand will lay hold of me. If I say, "Surely the darkness will overwhelm me, and the light around me will be night," even the darkness is not dark to You, and the night is as bright as the day. Darkness and light are alike to You (Ps. 139:7–12).

David the Psalmist knew what I should have realized when I was locked in that Chevy trunk: what is dark to me is clear as day to God. Even if no one on earth knew where I was, God knew. There is nowhere He cannot be, and there is nothing He cannot see.

God said to the prophet Jeremiah:

> "Am I only a God nearby," declares the LORD, "and not a God far away? Who can hide in secret

places so that I cannot see them?" declares the
Lord, "Do not I fill the heaven and earth?" declares
the Lord (Jer. 23:23–24; NIV).

The Scripture is clear that nothing gets past the notice
of the Creator: "Behold, He who keeps Israel will neither
slumber nor sleep" (Ps. 121:4).

In Matthew 10:29–30, Jesus tells us that His Father
is aware of every sparrow that drops from the sky, and
He keeps an exact count of the hairs of our head (which
changes daily for me!).

Hiding from God

Understanding all of this about God makes the next
story rather puzzling.

After Adam and Eve sinned in the garden, their eyes
were opened to the fact that they were naked. So they sewed
fig leaves together to make rather inadequate garments to
cover their bodies.

> And they heard the sound of the Lord God
> walking in the garden in the cool of the day, and the
> man and his wife hid themselves from the presence
> of the Lord God among the trees of the garden.
> Then the Lord God called to the man, and said to
> him, "Where are you?" (Gen. 3:8–9).

Based on everything we have learned about God from
previous verses, we can safely deduce that God is *not* asking
this question because He has no idea what has just taken

place and can't locate Adam amidst all of the trees! So, He isn't asking the question for His own benefit. The question is intended to help Adam. What was God wanting Adam to realize about himself and his condition?

> He [Adam] said, "I heard the sound of You in the garden, and I was afraid because I was naked; so I hid myself" (Gen. 3:10).

From this verse we can understand that Adam knew the sound of God walking in the garden. There was a close intimate knowledge that Adam had of the holy and the good. The Tree of the Knowledge of Good and Evil had not clued him into knowing what was good. He was already saturated in and surrounded by good. The only thing he gained when he partook of the forbidden fruit was an experiential knowledge of evil.

God is wanting Adam to feel the weight of the separation that has just occurred. That is why He calls. A second thing we can discern from verse 10 is that Adam expected God to come. He said he was afraid because of his nakedness and so he hid. Not only did he hide, but before he even heard the sound of their Creator in the garden, he and Eve had prepared garments to help cover their bodies. They knew God would come looking for them.

The openness and transparency they had in their relationship with Him is now shattered. No longer covered in the adequacy of what God had given them (which was being clothed in His image), now the man and the woman were trying to provide their own covering. No longer *being* righteous, they were trying to be content with *looking* righteous.

This act set the pattern for all of human existence. Not only do we try to hide our sin and keep God (and others) from knowing about it, but we dress ourselves up in our own righteousness hoping that it will be adequate to impress a Holy God. How foolish!

A Covering

> The LORD God made garments of skin for Adam and his wife, and clothed them (Gen 3:21).

Symbolically, God is showing them that He Himself will provide for them an adequate covering, but it will require the shedding of blood. No mere fig leaves of human ingenuity or craftiness will allow us to stand before God with a clear conscience. Sin cannot be hidden or concealed: there must be an atonement made.

God is well aware of our sin. Every thought and deed is before His eyes. We stand guilty before His gaze. We know that there will come a day when He will call our name and we will need to give an account for what we have done while in this body of flesh (Heb. 9:27).

Jesus told a parable in Matthew 22:11–14 about a man who came to the wedding feast (representing the final reuniting of the Creator and His creation) wearing his own garments and not the wedding garment provided by the king. He was thrown out into the darkness where there was "weeping and gnashing of teeth."

Paul declares in Philippians 3:3 that he puts no confidence in the flesh. Instead his hope is that he "may be found in [Christ], not having a righteousness of my own . . . but that which is through faith in Christ, the righteousness which comes from God on the basis of faith" (Phil. 3:9).

Again he says, "But *put on the Lord Jesus Christ*, and make no provision for the flesh in regard to its lusts" (Rom. 13:14; emphasis mine).

The good news (the gospel) is that we don't have to hide anymore. We don't have to try to provide a covering for ourselves to conceal our sin. Heaven forbid that we would choose a cloak of religiosity or a garment of our own goodness to make us look acceptable to our Maker! We would appear as pitiful as Adam and Eve in their crudely sewn fig leaves. Our own efforts to make ourselves acceptable are but filthy rags in God's sight (Isa. 64:6). Our garment of righteousness has been provided by the shed blood of Jesus Christ! What a perfect sacrifice! What a holy and blameless substitute! What a blessed promise of being reunited with our God! This is the amazing privilege to once again commune with Him and share sweet and intimate fellowship in the cool of the day.

So come out from where you have been hiding. Stop making excuses, shifting the blame, and pretending that you are okay. Admit that you have sinned and that you need a Savior. Our Father is more than willing to cover you in garments of righteousness and to welcome you into fellowship with Him. He sees, He knows, and He desires for you to see yourself as He does: rather silly and lonely, hiding in the leaves of your own goodness.

Chapter 3

Who Told You?

(Epistemology — Adam)

And He said, "Who told you that you were naked? Have you eaten from the tree of which I commanded you not to eat?"

— Genesis 3:11

Rene Descartes (1596–1650) was a French philosopher who one day thought so hard, he created a dilemma. He thought, as many of us have, about the odd fact that dreams seem to be very real when one is in the process of dreaming. It is only when one awakens that it becomes clear that the previous state of mind was a dream and not the real world.

So Descartes began to wonder if we could ever really be certain that we are, indeed, awake. Maybe we "wake up" from a dream (or so we think), but in reality we haven't awakened at all — we have merely awoken in another dream.

Then he began to wonder if we could be sure that we really exist, in a real world, or if everything is just an illusion. Maybe we only exist in another's dreams (God's dreams, for example). In his struggle to determine whether or not he existed, he finally made this famous dictum: *cogito ergo sum,* or "I think, therefore I am."

Like Descartes, I think too deeply at times. For example, I've often wondered this: if a philosopher were all alone in the woods, clapping using only one hand, would he still be impossible to understand?

How Do We Know What We Know?

The discipline of philosophy that Descartes was exploring (one that lays a foundation for all others) is called epistemology. This topic attempts to answer the question, "How do we *know* what we know?" or "What is the basis of knowledge?"

How do we know what is true? Is truth merely what I believe? Is it relative and different for all people, or is it objective and possible to apply to all people as a universal standard for truth?

There are many different approaches to epistemological questions and many different conclusions. Some of the books on the topic will make your head swim with their complexity. However, the topic can be simplified dramatically by considering that there are really only two voices in the universe that make truth claims. One is always right, and the other is always wrong (although Satan, the author of lies, incorporates an element of truth [which he twists and distorts] in his lies to make his arguments sound plausible).

The Beginning of Deception

In the Garden of Eden, Adam and his wife, Eve, had only one voice of information about the universe. It was the voice of pure, unadulterated truth. They heard from the very God who made all things and, therefore, understood intimately how everything worked. What they knew was true, good, and beautiful.

When they ate from the Tree of the Knowledge of Good and Evil, they didn't gain a knowledge of good and evil. They already knew good; they only gained a knowledge of evil. They were deceived by the words, "Did God really say. . . ?"

Prior to their sin, man and woman were completely honest and open before God and each other. There was no deception and no reason to fear or to hide. After sin entered the world, all of life took on a corrupting influence. Things that were previously good now had the potential for evil as well.

He said, "I heard the sound of You in the garden, and I was afraid because I was naked; so I hid myself." And He said, "Who told you that you were naked? Have you eaten from the tree of which I commanded you not to eat?" (Gen. 3:10–11).

God wanted Adam to be honest with himself. He wanted Adam to understand that his reaction was based on information that he obtained from a corrupt (and corrupting) source. Since that event, all throughout history, people have been faced with the choice of listening to one of these two voices that represent good or evil. Instead of becoming more like God, as the serpent promised, humans became more like Satan.

Today there are many philosophies that purport themselves to be avenues to higher knowledge and enlightenment. New Age, secular humanism, post-modernism, Eastern religions, Islamic fascism, atheism, naturalism, and other worldviews and philosophies surround us. All of these voices are just subsidiaries of the kingdom of this world. Satan has many paths and belief systems to choose from. He doesn't really care what you choose from the religious smorgasbord, as long as it isn't the truth. There is only one source of truth in the entire universe. Jesus said in John 14:6 that He is the Way, the Truth and Life. There is no way to come to the Father except through Him. The source of your information about life is crucial. Are you listening to the voice of good, or the voice of evil? When you examine your beliefs about life and reality, ask yourself this question, "Who told you?"

Chapter 4

Where Is Your Brother?

(Relationships — Cain)

Then the LORD said to Cain, "Where is Abel your brother?"

— Genesis 4:9

*E*t *tu, Brute?* "You too, Brutus?" According to Shakespeare's tragedy, Julius Caesar asked this question of the one man he thought he could trust. Despite Caesar's confidence in him, M. Junius Brutus was part of a conspiracy to murder the eminent ruler on March 15, 44 B.C. Have you ever wondered why it is so difficult to find true friends? Why is it that people can be so hurtful and treacherous? Brotherhood, in the first cause, has underscored the tension that humans have experienced throughout the ages.

In the original sin against God, Adam is asked, "Where are you?" (Gen. 3:9). In the first sin against humanity, Adam's son, Cain, is asked, "Where is your brother?"(Gen. 4:9). The issue undergirding both questions is love.

> "You shall love the Lord your God with all your heart, and with all your soul, and with all your mind, and with all your strength." The second is this, "You shall love your neighbor as yourself." There is no other commandment greater than these." The scribe said to Him, "Right, Teacher . . . to love one's neighbor as himself, is much more than all burnt offerings and sacrifices." When Jesus saw that he had answered intelligently, He said to him, "You are not far from the kingdom of God" (Mark 12:30–34).

While it is true that doctrines of salvation and justification are vertically oriented, every practical outworking of Christian sanctification is horizontal in its scope and application.

God isn't interested in our outward demonstrations of piety and liturgy; His desire is that we "do justice, to love kindness, and to walk humbly with our God" (Mic. 6:8).

> Woe to you, scribes and Pharisees, hypocrites! For you tithe mint and dill and cummin, and have neglected the weightier provisions of the law: justice and mercy and faithfulness; but these are the things you should have done without neglecting the others (Matt. 23:23).

Justice, mercy, and covenant faithfulness to God's people rank way above sacrifices and offerings. You can only consistently live this way if you are humble before the Lord, living in poverty of spirit. You can't think that your ideas, opinions, and desires must come before others around you. This was the lesson that Cain needed to learn.

God was pleased with Abel's sacrifice, but not with the offering of his older brother. Cain should have humbled himself before the Lord and sought to do the right thing. God assured Cain that he would be blessed if he assumed that posture (Gen. 4:7).

However, instead of recognizing that he could learn a thing or two from his younger brother, he viciously murdered him. Cain's callous heart is evident in his answer to God's question, "Where is Abel your brother?" Spewing hatred and venom, he retorted, "I do not know. Am I my brother's keeper?" (Gen. 4:9).

> For this is the message which you have heard from the beginning, that we should love one another; not as Cain, who was of the evil one and slew his brother. And for what reason did he slay him? Because his deeds were evil, and his brother's were righteous (1 John 3:11–12).

The saddest part of it all may be the fact that Cain "went out from the presence of the LORD" (Gen. 4:16). How many times have we seen, within the Body of Christ, a split among believers that ends in one or more parties completely walking away from the faith, in anger and disgust? The enemy of our souls — the tempter — is the accuser of the brethren (Rev. 12:10). We must never allow Satan to gain a foothold in our lives through bitterness. In as much as it lies within us, we need to live at peace with all men (Rom. 12:18).

> Therefore if you are presenting your offering at the altar, and there remember that your brother has something against you, leave your offering there before the altar and go; first be reconciled to your brother, and then come and present your offering (Matt. 5:23–24).

We must, of course, recognize that we can't control or be responsible for the actions of others. We can direct our own thoughts and actions, however, to ensure that they reflect the heart and character of our Savior.

Therefore if there is any encouragement in Christ, if there is any consolation of love, if there is any fellowship of the Spirit, if any affection and compassion, make my joy complete by being of the same mind, maintaining the same love, united in spirit, intent on one purpose. Do nothing from selfishness or empty conceit, but with humility of mind regard one another as more important than yourselves; do not merely look out for your own personal interests, but also for the interests of others (Phil. 2:1–4).

We need to be responsible siblings, looking out for the needs of those around us. In learning to love each other, we learn to love Christ. The way we treat those around us is, in effect, the way we treat Jesus Himself (Matt. 25:40). Before you say or do something to another brother or sister, ask yourself, "Would I say this about Jesus? Would I do this to Jesus?" Yes, I know that Jesus is perfect, so He wouldn't have been nasty to you, but keep in mind that He still loves the person who offends you. He commands you to love that person, even if he or she is your enemy. What he or she did may have been wrong. Maybe you were wrong. The point is, love has to undergird every word and action if the Lord is to be pleased with us.

He that saith he is in the light, and hateth his brother, is in darkness even until now (1 John 2:9; KJV).

We know that we have passed out of death into life, because we love the brethren. He who does not love abides in death. Everyone who hates his brother is a murderer; and you know that no murderer has eternal life abiding in him. We know love by this, that He laid down His life for us; and we ought to lay down our lives for the brethren (1 John 3:14–16).

No one has seen God at any time; if we love one another, God abides in us, and His love is perfected in us (1 John 4:12).

If someone says, "I love God," and hates his brother, he is a liar; for the one who does not love his brother whom he has seen, cannot love God whom he has not seen. And this commandment we have from Him, that the one who loves God should love his brother also" (1 John 4:20–21).

Just as God asked Cain about his brother, God is asking you and I about the condition of our heart as it relates to others. Is there anyone to whom you have withheld forgiveness? Is there anyone to whom you need to make confession and reconciliation? If so, don't wait another day to get it resolved. Do what it takes to be reunited in fellowship with your brother or sister.

Chapter 5

Why Are You Angry?

(Anger — Cain)

Then the Lord said to Cain, "Why are you angry?"

— Genesis 4:6

I recently received a letter from a man nearing 60 years old who is very bitter against his parents for issues in his childhood. His letter vented his seething anger and venom toward them. He refused to even refer to them as his father or mother, but instead he would use their first names or make reference to the "parents." His final statement was to insinuate that if he ever saw them again, it would be a murderous ordeal, necessitating SWAT teams and media crews.

The odd thing is that his parents are dearly loved by all of their other children, extended family, and friends. The man himself cannot really identify any justifiable cause for his anger and hostility. It makes me stop and ask myself, "What drives this kind of irrational anger: psychosis or evil?"

Some psychiatrists would lead us to believe that we are nothing more than biological creatures — that our behavior is determined strictly by chemical impulses that occur in the brain. Animals are creatures of instinct, and *determinism* teaches that we (as evolved animals) are creatures of instinct as well. According to some "experts," when we engage in "anti-social" behavior, we are merely acting according to our inner primal urgings (survival of the fittest).

This approach obviously seeks to relieve us of any responsibility for our own behavior. Worse yet, it may actually justify our negative actions toward others as being beneficial in some way to "the species," by creating a stronger race of people (kill off the weak so the strong will survive). If you have to step on others on your way to the top, so be it. This approach argues that there is no real "right" or "wrong" in terms of behavior; there are only "socially acceptable" and "socially unacceptable" actions.

Regardless of the appeal this philosophy may have, we all know instinctively that it is false. At least we do when someone commits a wrong against *us*! C.S. Lewis said, "Whenever you find a man who says he does not believe in a real Right and Wrong, you will find the same man going back on this a moment later. He may break his promise to you, but if you try breaking one to him he will be complaining 'It's not fair' before you can say 'Jack Robinson.' "[1]

There is another, more psychological approach called *behaviorism*, which teaches that we are born innately good (or at least morally neutral), and it is society or our social environment that makes us do bad things. So again, what we do is not our fault; we are victims of external stimuli.

The Bible is not silent on this issue. Let's look at Cain as an example of negative, "anti-social" behavior. Cain's anger is one of the first sinful responses recorded in the Bible. As Cain and his brother, Abel, brought their offerings to the Lord, Cain found his feeble attempt to please God disregarded and rejected. This is where personal responsibility should have kicked in. Cain only had three options:

- Admit that he was the problem and that his heart and actions needed to change.

1. C.S. Lewis, *Mere Christianity* (New York: HarperCollins Publishers, 1980), p. 6.

35

- Blame Abel for Cain's personal failure.
- Blame God for having an unfair standard.

Cain chose the latter two. Cain became angry and sullen.

> Then the LORD said to Cain, "Why are you angry? And why has your countenance fallen? If you do well, will not your countenance be lifted up? And if you do not do well, sin is crouching at the door; and its desire is for you, but you must master it" (Gen. 4:6–7).

We never just "fall into" sin. Before we sin, we always face an internal war in our mind and soul. Often we view ourselves as victims of some external force that bends our will in one direction or another, taking us captive to some unavoidable wrongdoing. However, it is only when we have done something that we know intuitively is immoral, that we purport to have no will or choice in the matter. "It's only our bad temper that we put down to being tired or worried or hungry; we put our good temper down to ourselves."[2]

> Let no one say when he is tempted, "I am being tempted by God"; for God cannot be tempted by evil, and He Himself does not tempt anyone. But each one is tempted when he is carried away and enticed *by his own lust*. Then when lust has

---

2. Ibid., p. 8.

conceived, it gives birth to sin; and when sin is accomplished, it brings forth death (James 1:13–15; emphasis mine).

We all feel justified in venting our anger at others, and yet when we are the recipients of someone else's rage, we feel hurt and believe that we are unappreciated and misunderstood.

What causes fights and quarrels among you? Don't they come from *your desires* that battle within you? You desire but do not have, so you kill. You covet but you cannot get what you want, so you quarrel and fight. You do not have because you do not ask God. When you ask, you do not receive, because you ask with wrong motives, that you may spend what you get on your pleasures" (James 4:1–3; NIV, emphasis mine).

Lest we think that our anger against others isn't a big deal, look at Jesus' words in Matthew 5:22: "But I say unto you, that whosoever is angry with his brother without a cause shall be in danger of the judgment" (KJV). Cain's problem had nothing to do with his brother. Abel was minding his own business, trying to please the Lord and live at peace with all men. Cain, on the other hand, was eaten up by his own evil desires and bitterness. When you allow lies to live in your mind (especially if you nurture and cultivate them), sin grows like a cancer inside of you, eating out the very core of your soul. When you are bitter or angry, you die a slow, painful death, one breath at a time. Your poisonous attitude also brings death to others, either emotionally or sometimes physically.

The way out of the trap of anger is repentance and asking God to give you a new heart, a heart like His. "'Even now,' declares the LORD, 'return to me with all your heart, with fasting and weeping and mourning.' Rend your heart and not your garments. Return to the LORD your God, for He is gracious and compassionate, *slow to anger* and abounding in love, and He relents from sending calamity" (Joel 2:12–13; NIV, emphasis mine). There is absolutely no sin that cannot be forgiven, nor from which you cannot be delivered if you place it in the hands of the Almighty God and are willing to walk out the steps of brokenness and repentance that He requires.

- The first step is to acknowledge before God and men that your anger problem is your own fault.
- The second step is to admit that your anger is inexcusable and must be forsaken.
- Next you must confess your sin to God and repent from your heart to those you have hurt by your attitudes and actions. They may not forgive you. That isn't your responsibility. You simply need to humble yourself and do your part. Let God work in the hearts of those you have hurt.
- You should confess your sin to other believers who can keep you accountable and help counsel you regarding changes you need to make in your attitude

and behavior. They can only help you if you really want help, so don't play games with them. Be real and welcome their advice and rebuke if it is needed.

- Learn to walk in a constant state of brokenness and humility. It is your pride and self-centeredness that causes you to demand your rights. Your anger is based out of a selfish desire to control others and see everything go your way. Die to that carnal pride. Other people and their needs are more important than you and your needs. If you blow it, quickly repent to keep your heart soft and pliable before God.

- Ask God, by His Holy Spirit, to change your heart. You can't do this on your own. You need divine intervention. You can't manage your anger through sheer willpower. You are the problem, not the solution.

You don't have to live as a slave to your passions and temper. You can and must become free for the sake of the glory of God and His perfect plan for your life.

Chapter 6

Where Is Your Wife?

(Marriage — Abraham)

"Where is Sarah your wife?"

— Genesis 18:9

I magine living for nearly 100 years and being deprived of something your heart had longed for more than anything. Suppose you had a hope or a dream that seemed just out of reach. This was the case for Abraham the patriarch.

Proverbs 13:12 says, "Hope deferred makes the heart sick, but desire fulfilled is a tree of life." His original name, "Abram," means "exalted father." The new name God gave him, "Abraham," means "father of many." In the Old Testament, a person's name often summed up the core of that person's existence. Everything about Abraham spoke of his destiny as the father of many nations.

Guests

On a very ordinary day, Abraham received a visit from three unexpected guests. He ran to meet them and bowed low to the earth. He offered them lunch and begged them to stay, which they did. Two of the "men" were angels (see Gen. 19:1), and the other was YHWH (God) Himself, manifested in human form (see Gen. 18:1, 22)!

Ever have people stop by your house unexpectedly? That can be a real test of hospitality! I don't know about you, but I think I would have had a panic attack trying to think of preparing lunch for *these* guests! I'm not sure what was going through Abraham's mind, but perhaps he was in a panic as well. He immediately went to find Sarah in the tent and asked her to make the equivalent of 35 loaves of bread! Then he had his servants prepare a choice, tender calf. Next he served them some milk and cottage cheese, which they ate. While they were snacking under a tree, Abraham stood nearby watching them.

I think I would do the same thing. I'd be pinching myself thinking, *I didn't think supernatural beings could eat food. This is amazing!* Whatever Abraham's thoughts, they were interrupted by this question, "Where is Sarah your wife?" (Gen. 18:9).

"There, in the tent," he answered.

Okay, let's stop for a minute here. Did the Almighty God, the Creator of the universe, lose track of Sarah? Did He not realize that she was nearby, probably still kneading dough for all those loaves of bread her husband had ordered? Of course He knew!

So, who is the question intended for? It is for Abraham. What is God trying to get Abraham to realize or understand? Let's look at what happens next.

> He [the Lord] said, "I will surely return to you at this time next year; and behold, Sarah your wife will have a son'" (Gen. 18:10).

The Bible tells us that Sarah was standing at the entrance to the tent, behind the Lord. She knew that she couldn't be seen or heard, so she laughed to herself and thought, "After I have become old, shall I have pleasure?" (verse 12). She didn't even say it out loud. She just let the thought go through her mind.

> And the LORD said to Abraham, "Why did Sarah laugh, saying, 'Shall I indeed bear a child,

when I am so old?' Is anything too difficult for the Lord?" (Gen. 18:13).

It is important to note that He didn't ask Sarah why she laughed, but instead He asked Abraham. Why ask Abraham? How should he know why his wife laughed? Is it his fault or responsibility that she laughed?

He then reaffirms His promise that upon His return, one year later, Abraham and Sarah would be holding their newborn son.

When her lack of faith was exposed, Sarah quickly tried to cover it up by lying. "I did not laugh," she stated. But the Lord said to her, "No, but you did laugh" (Gen. 18:15).

Leadership

Okay, so why is Abraham being questioned about Sarah and her behavior? It all goes back to a principle of leadership that God established with the first couple. Just as Adam was passive, allowing his wife to take the lead in listening to the serpent and eating the forbidden fruit (see Gen. 3), so husbands throughout time have failed to take the lead in their homes.

Abraham is one of these passive men. Yes, he is featured in Hebrews 11. Yes, he is often called "the father of faith." Yet when you look closely at his relationship with Sarah, he often lets her shoulder the responsibility for leadership.

To begin with, he is afraid that the heathens in the land will try to kill him and take his beautiful wife to be their own. However, instead of being a man about it, he puts the pressure on his wife to lie in order to protect him. Wives should never be placed in the position of having to protect their husbands.

Secondly, we see in Genesis 16 that Sarai (her name at that point) was discouraged regarding God's promise. She suggested to Abram that perhaps God intended to fulfill His plan in some metaphorical sense. She acted like many today who say, "Maybe you can't interpret that Scripture as being literal." So she suggests that Abram take Hagar, Sarai's servant, and fulfill the promise through her (as though God needed help implementing His plan!).

Abram is not a potted plant here. He was the patriarch of his household. He could have nixed that plan, but instead of being a leader, he chose the role of a follower. The past 4,000 years of conflict in the Middle East between the descendants of Isaac and Ishmael have told the bloody story of that fatal decision.

In chapter 17 of Genesis, the Lord appears to Abram to give him the details of the covenantal promise regarding Isaac. In verse 5, God changes his name to Abraham, and in verses 15 and 16 He instructs Abraham, "As for Sarai your wife, you shall not call her name Sarai, but Sarah shall be her name. I will bless her, and indeed I will give you a son by her. Then I will bless her, and she shall be a mother of nations; kings of peoples will come from her."

In the very next verse Abraham laughed and began to express doubt regarding the promise. He suggested to God that it would be a lot easier if God would simply bless the plan that he and his wife had already worked out. . . that of

Ishmael. In verse 21, God is emphatic: "But My covenant I will establish with Isaac, whom Sarah will bear to you at this season next year." No "ifs, ands, or buts"; God is going to do things His way.

Now put yourself in Abraham's shoes for a minute. Tonight when he goes back to the tent with his wife, he is no longer going to call her "Sarai." He has called her by that name for the past 89 years. This was not going to be an easy habit to break. Not only that, he needed to explain to her that she must now call him, "Abraham." Why? Well, because God has changed their names as a result of His promise regarding their future son, Isaac. Every time they would call each other by their new names, they would be reminding one another of God's covenant promise.

I don't know how much time lapsed between God's appearance to Abraham in chapter 17 and the three visitors in chapter 18, but it was less than a year, perhaps weeks. (Compare 17:21 with 18:10.) There was enough time to give Abraham ample time to bring his wife up to speed on the promise. If Abraham had been a proper leader, he would have approached Sarah somewhat like this: "Sarah, your name, which means 'Princess,' indicates God's favor toward you. You are blessed. In about one year's time you are going to have a son. Not just any son, but God says this is a son of promise. God says you are going to be the mother of nations, and kings will come from your womb! Let's go to Gerar and buy all the blue baby clothes they have!"

I don't believe he did that. Wives often respond very similarly to their husbands in situations like this. God ordained husbands to lead and wives to follow. Because her heart had not been truly built up in faith and trust by her husband, Sarah responded just as he had in 17:17, with laughter and unbelief. God didn't scold her (until she lied and tried to deceive Him), but instead he looks straight at Abraham and asks, "Why did Sarah laugh?" It is notable that God uses her new name, which is linked with His promise.

Modern-Day Patriarchs

Even faithful men of God who do admirably in many areas of their lives fall down in the area of leading their wives. That is why Paul in 1 Timothy 3:11 requires of deacons, "In the same way, the women are to be worthy of respect, not malicious talkers but temperate and trustworthy in everything" (NIV).

In Ephesians 5:22–33, Paul once again tells husbands to love their wives in the same way Christ loves the Church. Part of this love is demonstrated in a man's faithfulness to use the Word of God as a means of cleansing and sanctifying his wife in her spiritual life, just as he allows the Word to cleanse his own life. This must not be done with a superior attitude, but with gentleness, in the same manner in which Christ laid down His life for the Church (thought of her needs above His own).

Husbands, likewise, dwell with them with understanding, giving honor to the wife, as to the weaker vessel, and as being heirs together of the grace of life, that your prayers may not be hindered" (1 Pet. 3:7; NKJV).

Men, you need to be an "heir of the grace of life" with your wife. In your pursuit, however, you must not forget that you are to lead and your wife is to follow your lead. Don't leave her guessing about the direction you are heading. Don't expect her to take the lead and make the major decisions of life. There are way too many wimpy men who look out for their own interests and neglect to faithfully shelter and spiritually nurture their wives.

Where is your wife? Where is she spiritually? Where is she emotionally? Is her life being enhanced and benefitted spiritually because of your influence as her husband? Are you on one track and she on another? Does she know what you have received from the Lord regarding direction for your family? Does she know that you are not only hearing from God yourself on a regular basis, but that you are faithfully transmitting what you are learning to her and your children? If you are not lovingly leading your wife, you are disobeying God (which is a sin). If you, like Abraham, are feeling the awkward guilt of failing to lead your wife in faith, repent and move forward in humble obedience. God will bless you, just as He did the "father of faith" over 4,000 years ago.

Chapter 7

Is Anything Too Difficult for the Lord?

(Faith — Abraham and Sarah)

And the LORD said to Abraham, "Why did Sarah laugh, saying, 'Shall I indeed bear a child, when I am so old?' Is anything too difficult for the LORD? At the appointed time I will return to you, at this time next year, and Sarah shall have a son."

— Genesis 18:13–14

ngus Buchan, a farmer in South Africa, underwent a great personal transformation. Redeemed from a life of selfish ambition and a violent temper, he surrendered to Jesus Christ and became a sold-out witness for the Lord. Angus Buchan is an example of a simple man, with a simple faith, who has accomplished great things through faith in God.

His story has been published in a book entitled *Faith Like Potatoes* and also in a film that was released in 2009. One of the main statements on which he has based his life is that miracles do not happen when things are difficult, but rather when the situation is *impossible*!

That was the situation in which Abraham found himself. God had made a promise that his wife, Sarah, would have a child and that God would make from him a great nation. The facts were that Abraham was 100 years old, and Sarah was 90. Beyond that, Sarah was barren, and had been since they were first married. This was not merely difficult; this was biologically impossible.

For those who operate within a rationalistic framework, only the natural or physical is possible. Modernism has promoted the idea that we are merely biological machines operating within a closed system. However, as Christians, we believe not only in the natural, but the supernatural. We believe that God can do all of His sovereign will.

The key is the will of God. We need to know and understand what is the will of God — His good, pleasing, and perfect will. We obtain the knowledge of His will by living in total surrender to God, coming under His leadership, being obedient to Him, and humbly seeking direction from His Word.

> This is the confidence which we have before Him, that, if we ask anything according to His will, He hears us. And if we know that He hears us in whatever we ask, we know that we have the requests which we have asked from Him (1 John 5:14–15).

If God has it in His heart to do something, nothing in heaven, earth, or hell itself can stand against Him. Yet God does not often act alone in the universe. He invites us to join Him in what He is doing. He often chooses frail humans as objects of His mercy so that He can demonstrate His power through them. The blessing is to participate with Him in His plan. The challenge is to walk by faith, fully expecting Him to do what He has promised.

This approach is the complete opposite of how we usually approach life. We usually charge ahead with our ideas and agenda, and only after we have begun building a house do we ask God to bless it (Ps. 127:1). Instead, we need to listen, ask, seek, and knock to discover where God is working, and then ask to join Him in His work. This is a principle which Henry Blackaby teaches well in his study called *Experiencing God*.

This is not a process of "name it, claim it," "blab it, grab it" Christianity, where we act like a spoiled brat in a toy store. God is not under any obligation to give us anything or to use us in any way. If He does, it is an act of His sovereign grace and mercy. Seeing the impossible become possible is obtaining, by faith, what has already been revealed by God to be His will.

The struggle that I often face is thinking erroneously that God cannot do anything that I cannot do. If something is too difficult for me to do without God, then I somehow assume that it is too difficult for God to do through me. You can open your Bible virtually anywhere to quickly see the fallacy of this kind of thinking. God seldom chose people with exceptional abilities, but rather those who had no strengths of their own.

> For consider your calling, brethren, that there were not many wise according to the flesh, not many mighty, not many noble; but God has chosen the foolish things of the world to shame the wise, and God has chosen the weak things of the world to shame the things which are strong, and the base things of the world and the despised God has chosen, the things that are not, that He may nullify the things that are, so that no man may boast before God (1 Cor. 1:26–29).

The idea is that God wants to glorify Himself, not us. He wants to get all of the credit. If our situation were merely difficult, we could take pride in the fact that we "somehow" pulled it out and made it happen. If it were merely difficult, we could have a naturalistic explanation for how the situation remedied itself without divine intervention. However, when the situation is *impossible*, that is when God will come through and do what only He can do.

That is what God did for Abraham and Sarah. That is what God is willing to do for you if you trust Him to lead you! Are you ready to join Him on your next "Mission Impossible"?

Chapter 8

What Is Your Name?

(Honesty — Jacob)

So he said to him, "What is your name?"

— Genesis 32:27

Whan I was a child, there was a business in our town called "Honest Eddy's Used Cars." I don't know how that title hits you, but if you have to put the word "honest" in the title of your business . . . I'm just sayin'! I could just imagine Eddy puffing on his cigar telling a prospective customer a whopper of a tale about whatever piece of junk he had just pulled off the auction block.

"Yes sir, 15,000 original miles on this 18-year-old sedan! Drives like a champ! You can't go wrong!"

There are some people who just seem determined to take the crooked path.

A Liar

In Genesis 25, we are introduced to the Old Testament's version of "Honest Eddy." Rebekah gave birth to twins, and the younger twin was born grasping the heel of the older, so they named him "Jacob," which means "one who grasps the heel," or figuratively, "deceiver" or "liar." I'm pretty sure this led to his older brother, Esau, constantly needing to ask his childhood twin, "Are you pulling my leg again?!"

In biblical times, names often held a prophetic significance. It seems that people often lived up to the names their parents gave them. This could be a blessing or a tyranny (as seen in the case of Jabez, in 1 Chronicles 4).

A Legacy

In terms of the issue of deception, it seems that the odds were stacked against Jacob. Consider these examples of deception exhibited by his ancestors and relatives:

- Abraham (Gen. 20:1–2)
- Sarah (Gen. 18:15)
- Isaac (Gen. 26:6–7)
- Rebekah (Gen. 27:5–17)
- Uncle Laban (Gen. 29:25–26; 31:7, 13–14)

Whether as a result of nature or nurture, Jacob seems doomed to a lifestyle of deceit and treachery. Not only did Jacob come from a heritage of deception, his parents also made the mistake of playing favorites with their sons. Sadly, Jacob continued this trend as well, favoring his two youngest sons: Joseph and Benjamin. It is a well-demonstrated fact that many people have a difficult time transcending the lessons they learned from their parents. That is as it should be, but sometimes, if the influence of the parents is negative, it can be hard to chart a different course.

Seeking a Blessing

It seems that the primary pursuit of Jacob's life was seeking to be blessed. Jacob was constantly trying to work circumstances and situations around to ensure that he would come out on the best end of any deal. He conspired to take the birthright (inheritance) from his brother, Esau (see Gen. 25:29–34). He then managed to take away the blessing of the firstborn as well. He wanted life to go his way.

The Lord, *Your* God

It is very interesting to look at a couple of features in the exchange between Jacob and his father, Isaac.

Then he came to his father and said, "My father." And he said, "Here I am. Who are you, my son?" Jacob said to his father, "I am Esau your first-born; I have done as you told me. Get up, please, sit and eat of my game, that you may bless me." Isaac said to his son, "How is it that you have it so quickly, my son?" And he said, "Because the LORD *your God* caused it to happen to me" (Gen. 27:18–20; emphasis mine).

Being the child of a godly parent doesn't make one a godly person. At this point in his life, Jacob has not yet internalized the faith of his fathers. He is trusting in his own cunning and ability rather than on the power and grace of God.

My Name Is Esau

In seeking a blessing from his father, Isaac, Jacob uses deception. Jacob plays on his father's blindness and says that he is Esau, defrauding his brother once again.

Then Isaac said to Jacob, "Please come close, that I may feel you, my son, whether you are really my son Esau or not." So Jacob came close to Isaac his father, and he felt him and said, "The voice is the voice of Jacob, but the hands are the hands of Esau." He did not recognize him, because his hands were hairy like his brother Esau's hands; so he blessed him. And he said, "Are you really my son Esau?"

And he said, "I am." So he said, "Bring it to me, and I will eat of my son's game, that I may bless you" (Gen. 27:21–25).

This pattern of deception eventually ends up spreading from Jacob to his future family:

- Rachel steals her father's idols and hides them (Gen. 31:34–35).
- Jacob's sons dip Joseph's coat in blood and deceive their father (Gen. 37:31–32).

We receive a heritage from our parents and ancestors. We usually receive a mixture of good and bad. But what do you do when that heritage is mostly negative? You have to forge a new trail.

Finding His Own Faith

The road to relationship with God is long and drawn out for Jacob. It begins when he journeys to the land of his Uncle Laban, in search of a bride — and plenty of distance between him and the brother who wants him dead.

In Genesis 28:10–18, God shows up and introduces Himself to Jacob. While Jacob is asleep, using a stone for a pillow, he has a dream. He sees angels ascending and descending up and down a ladder that reaches up to heaven. Then God, who stood above the ladder, spoke:

"I am the Lord, the God of your father Abraham and the God of Isaac; the land on which you lie, I will give it to you and to your descendants. Your descendants will also be like the dust of the earth, and you will spread out to the west and to the east and to the north and to the south; and in you and in your descendants shall all the families of the earth be blessed. Behold, I am with you and will keep you wherever you go, and will bring you back to this land; for I will not leave you until I have done what I have promised you" (Gen. 28:13–15).

God gives Jacob some historical context. He reminds Jacob of the covenant he had made to Abraham and then to Isaac, and He renews that covenant with Jacob.

Then Jacob awoke from his sleep. . . and said, "How awesome is this place! This is none other than the house of God, and this is the gate of heaven" (Gen. 28:16–17).

So he changed the name of the place from Luz, to Bethel, which means "The House of God." This is the beginning of Jacob's personal walk with God. In my mind, this event is similar to what many people experience when they go to an evangelistic meeting, hear the gospel, and respond to an altar call. Jacob responds to God, but he does so very conditionally. He has a very self-focused approach to his relationship with God. Notice the great big "if" in the following passage:

Then Jacob made a vow, saying, "If God will be with me and will keep me on this journey that I take, and will give me food to eat and garments to wear, and I return to my father's house in safety, then the LORD will be my God. This stone, which I have set up as a pillar, will be God's house, and of all that You give me I will surely give a tenth to You" (Gen. 28:20–22).

To put it in the modern-day vernacular, if God will feed him, clothe him, keep him safe, and not let anything bad happen to him, then he will follow God, go to church, and tithe. Sound familiar? Not too different than much of modern-day American Christianity.

A Long Road Home

The next 20 years found Jacob marrying his true love, Rachel, her sister Leah (he was conned by his father-in-law, Laban, who proved to be a conniving match for Jacob), fathering 12 sons and 1 daughter, and working to pay off his debts for them and his own flocks.

This is a rough and bumpy season for Jacob. He really struggles with his relationships and I think with his own personal desires. The man wants to be blessed. Any dreams he has had of easy health, wealth, and prosperity are slow in coming. He is visited again in a dream by the Angel of the Lord, who tells him to pack up his things and head to his homeland (see Gen. 31:9–13).

Rather than deal with the painful conflict that will emerge in trying to talk things out with his father-in-law, he just loads up the family, their servants and belongings, and heads out in the middle of the night.

The Camp of God

After being pursued by Laban and making an agreement to part in peace, Jacob arrives at the Jabbok River. God meets with Jacob once again. Jacob set up another altar and names the place *Mahanaim*, which means "two camps," declaring this is the camp of God.

As Jacob approached Esau, he assumed his brother was probably still angry over the little "swindle your brother out of everything he owns" stunt. In preparation for meeting with his brother Esau, Jacob decided to make a peace offering. Hearing that Esau was approaching with 400 armed men (a standard militia in those days) confirmed his worst fears, so he divided his entourage into two camps. He sent the servants with their possessions ahead of his family, along with a large gift of livestock. Then he sent Leah and her children, and finally Rachel and her children. He had them all cross over the river while he stayed on the safe side of the river.

I find his rationale on this to be very intriguing. He says, "If Esau comes to the one company and attacks it, then the company which is left will escape" (Gen. 32:8).

He sends what is least valuable to him first, so that those who are in the back can escape if things go bad. The irony is that he stays on the safe side of the river (presumably so he can get away if no one else does?)! This is not exactly manliness and chivalry at its finest. Personally, I love how the Bible is so honest. This transparency into the failures of its heroes gives it a unique ring of authenticity.

Wrestling with God

That night, Jacob is all alone. He cries out to God, reminding God of His promises and asking for deliverance. A "man" engages Jacob and begins to wrestle with him all through the night until daybreak. This is no ordinary human (Gen. 32:30). Jacob has just encountered the living God (theologians call this "a theophany" when God takes the form of a human).

As they struggle, the man touches Jacob's hip socket and it is wrenched out of joint. This will not deter Jacob. He is intent on getting from God what He has promised.

Then (the man) said, "Let me go, for the dawn is breaking." But (Jacob) said, "I will not let you go unless you bless me" (Gen. 32:26).

As a side note, in the original Hebrew language, there is a nice little play on words here. Jacob (*ya'aqob*), wrestled (*ye'abeq*) at Jabbok (*yabboq* "yab-boke" — wrestler).

A Name Change

In the midst of this intense physical struggle, from out of nowhere comes an unexpected question: "So he said to him, 'What is your name?' " (Gen. 32:27).

What is the point of this question? Does God make a point of getting into random fights with unknown strangers in the middle of the night? Wasn't this a divine appoint-ment? Is God having an amnesia attack and suddenly can't remember the name of this guy? Who is this question for? It's either for God or for Jacob.

I believe the secret in understanding this question is all in the context. You have to remember that the last time Jacob asked his earthly father for a blessing, he lied. He said his name was Esau. Now, after all this time, God wants Jacob to finally be honest with himself and with God. Jacob finally gives in and fully surrenders to God: "And he said, 'Jacob' " (Gen. 32:27). It is as if he is finally owning up to what kind of person he has been — "I'm a liar. I'm a deceiver." It is at this point that God demonstrates grace in response to Jacob's humility.

"He said, 'Your name shall no longer be Jacob, but Israel; for you have striven with God and with men and have prevailed" (Gen. 32:28). Only God can change some-one from being a chronic liar to a "prince with God."

> Then Jacob asked him and said, "Please tell me your name." But he said, "Why is it that you ask my name?" And he blessed him there. So Jacob named the place Peniel, for he said, "I have seen God face to face, yet my life has been preserved." Now the sun rose upon him just as he crossed over Penuel, and he was limping on his thigh (Gen. 32:29–31).

Jacob left this encounter a changed man. This time he didn't put up an altar of remembrance, because he took one with him. He left limping, having a daily reminder of this struggle and his need to avoid relying on the strength of his own human flesh. He moved from a "Bethel" relationship with God, where he merely came into God's house on occasion when it was convenient and things were going well, to a "Peniel" relationship, where he now lived "in the face" or presence of God.

Being a Blessing

Instead of wanting to "have" a blessing, now Jacob's life is defined by wanting to "be" a blessing. He goes to make things right with his brother, but this time he leads the way, going ahead of his servants and family, the way a godly leader should (see Gen. 33:3). Jacob acknowledged in Genesis 33:5 that everything that he had received was a result of the favor of God. He no longer had a need to try to control his own circumstances. He had found God to be a faithful provider.

At the end of Jacob's life, when he is an old man, we see him blessing the mighty pharaoh (Gen. 47:7), his own son, and grandsons (Gen. 48). What a powerful testimony of a life transformed.

What Is Your Name?

Since God has recorded the account of Jacob wrestling with God in the Bible, and included that poignant question, we now need to ask, "What does this mean to us?"

What are some of the besetting sins that you have fought in your life? Are there sins that seem to have transferred from generation to generation through your family? What would it take to start your own spiritual legacy of faithfulness, rather than faithlessness? Are you relying completely on God's grace to provide for you and meet your needs, or are you trusting in your own cunning and human effort? Are there people with whom you need to seek reconciliation and restitution? Are you ready to have your identity changed from one of carnality to one of true spirituality?

What is your name?

Chapter 9

What Is in Your Hand?

(Service — Moses)

The LORD said to him, "What is that in your hand?"

— Exodus 4:2

The cure for a self-reliant heart is sometimes very painful. In order for God to use you effectively in His kingdom work, you need to be stripped of your own over-exalted view of your ability. God is quite capable of doing this, but the process is often severe and intense.

Moses was a man who was raised with a sense of leadership. He was rescued from the Nile by the pharaoh's daughter and raised in the palace as a prince. At that time, Egypt was the most powerful economic and political force on earth. Moses would have doubtless seen the richest rulers of the world come to the courts of pharaoh to seek alliances, trade . . . or beg mercy.

As you remember, a time came when Moses no longer sought to align himself with the riches and power afforded by the Egyptian dynasty, but rather to join his heart with the people of God (Heb. 11:23–29). In his effort to show his allegiance to his own people, he struck down an Egyptian, killing him, and forcing him to flee and live in the wilderness as a shepherd for the next 40 years.

Sometimes people have a sense of God's call on their life, but they jump the gun, so to speak. Instead of waiting for the Lord to open the door in His own time, they rush ahead and try to accomplish God's purposes in their own strength.

God is very jealous for His own glory. He will not allow another to receive the honor and praise for what is due to Him alone. Therefore, He resists the proud and shows favor to those who are lowly and humble before Him.

Something Is Going to Humble You

When we catch up with Moses, 40 years later, he is no longer a hothead who is full of himself and confident in his own abilities (see Exod. 3:1–6, 11–15). It's amazing how spending four decades chasing sheep can let the air out of your pride balloon. If anything, Moses is now on the other end of the self-esteem spectrum.

When God speaks to him from the burning bush, revealing His plan to bring liberation to the people of Israel, Moses is not enthusiastic to sign up. Moses asks God three questions that reveal his reticence to obey.

Doubting Yourself

The first question Moses asks God is, "Who am I?" (Exod. 3:11). Moses committed the fallacy of thinking it was all about him. The problem with low self-esteem is that the focus is *still* in the wrong place: *self*! In reality, it wasn't about who Moses was. He used to be a somebody, but now he was a nobody. The fact is the job was way over Moses' ability. He had proven that to himself 40 years before. However, God wasn't asking about his ability . . . but his availability.

Doubting God

The next question Moses asks God is, in essence, "Who are You?" (Exodus 3:13). It's one thing for Moses to doubt his own credentials and ability. It's another to start questioning God's! The name through which God reveals Himself, "I

AM that I AM," reflects God's all-sufficiency and infinity. God was here before Moses or pharaoh, and He will remain long after they are gone. There is no lack in God.

Fear of Man

Finally, Moses asks God, "What if they will not believe me?" (Exod. 4:1). If we aren't doubting ourselves or doubting God, we are thinking about our reputation. We are worried about what others will think of us. We are afraid of looking foolish, or of being laughed at or ridiculed if we fail. At this point, Moses wasn't worried about the reputation of God's honor and glory, though he was later as seen in Numbers 14:13–16. He was concerned about his own reputation.

From the Ordinary to the Extraordinary

Just as Jesus in the New Testament often answered His questioners with a question, so God "answers" Moses: "What is that in your hand?" (Exod. 4:2–4). Moses answered, "A rod." There was nothing special about the rod. It was an ordinary, lifeless stick. God told Moses to throw down the rod, and it turned into a snake. Frightened, Moses ran from the snake (as we might expect!).

There is an important principle here. When you take what you have, dead and lifeless though it may be, and give it to God, it becomes living and sometimes even a bit scary. It is not uncommon for the call of God on your life to be outside of the scope of your comfort zone. As C.S. Lewis put it in *The Chronicles of Narnia*, our God is neither tame nor safe!

"Ooh!" said Susan, "I thought he was a man. Is he quite safe? I shall feel rather nervous about meeting a lion."

"That you will, dearie, and no mistake," said Mrs. Beaver, "if there's anyone who can appear before Aslan without their knees knocking, they're either braver than most or else silly."

"Then he isn't safe?" said Lucy.

"Safe?" said Mr. Beaver. "Don't you hear what Mrs. Beaver tells you? Course he isn't safe. But he's good. He's the king, I tell you."[1]

Brother Andrew, the founder of Open Doors Ministries and author of the Christian classic *God's Smuggler*, once said, "If your vision doesn't scare you, your vision is too small, and so is your God!"

No Confidence in the Flesh

Immediately following the miracle of the rod, God told Moses to put his hand in his cloak. It became leprous. Forty years before, Moses had sought to bring deliverance for God's people with the strength of his own hand. I believe this miracle was to demonstrate to Moses that deliverance was not going to be in the power of his own hand, or his own fleshly effort. It was going to be in the power of God, which was symbolized by the rod that Moses held in his hand.

---

1. Excerpt from C.S. Lewis, *The Lion, the Witch and the Wardrobe* (New York: HarperCollins, 1994).

What Does the Rod Represent?

The rod represents God's provision and deliverance. There are several principles of the rod that are instructive for us today.

1. The rod is dead and lifeless until God acts upon (and empowers) it.
2. The rod must be voluntarily given to God for His purposes.
3. The rod is something ordinary that we have in our possession.
4. The rod is something that we know how to use.
5. The rod is not typically costly or hard to obtain.
6. The rod is unnoticed until God brings it to our attention.
7. The rod is almost always used for the deliverance and provision of *others*.

From the time that Moses turns over ownership of the rod for Kingdom work, it is thence called "The Rod of God." It was used by God to part the waters of the Red Sea, draw water from a rock, to bring the plague of locusts, bring down thunder, fire, and hail, bring a victory over the Amalekites, and much more.

Once Given, You Don't Get It Back

If you give something to God (your talents, your finances, your time, your business, your home, etc.), be assured that God now considers it His! He doesn't want you to take it back and use it for your own purposes (as Moses did when he struck the rock in Numbers 20:11).

The story has a bit of a sad ending in one sense. The last time we read of the staff is in Numbers 20:6–13. Moses is instructed to speak, the very thing he is told to do in the first place. But instead, he uses God's staff for his own purposes and uses the mouth God gave him for himself. The staff disappears from the biblical record. One of the most iconic symbols of deliverance in the Bible, Moses' staff, vanishes without a trace after it was used for human glory.

Let this be a warning to us to live only for our King. Let God use what is in your hand for His glory, to accomplish His purposes.

Whatever your hand finds to do, do it with all your might (Eccles. 9:10).

So What Is in Your Hand?

Let's look at a few of the other times when God used something common and ordinary for the deliverance and/or provision of/for His people.

1. David: a slingshot and five smooth stones (1 Sam. 7:38–40)
2. Gideon's fleece: a sign for direction (Judg. 6:36–38)
3. Gideon's army: a torch, a clay pot, and a trumpet (Judg. 7:16)
4. Samson: a donkey's jawbone. Killed 1,000 Philistines (Judg. 15:15)

5. The widow of Zarepheth: a handful of flour and a little oil (1 Kings 19:8–16)
6. Elijah: a robe, to part the waters of the river (2 Kings 2:8, 14)
7. Elisha: a new bowl of salt to purify the water (2 Kings 2:20–22)
8. Elisha: a bit of flour to redeem the poisonous soup (2 Kings 4:38–44)
9. Elisha: a stick thrown into the water to cause a borrowed axehead to float (2 Kings 6:6)
10. The Disciples: a little boy's loaves and fish to feed thousands (John 6:9)
11. Jesus: water into wine (John 2:1–11)

Following Is Not a Formula!

Instead of trying to manufacture a miracle by finding specific objects, gifts, and talents to give to God, surrender everything you have and give it to God (since it all belongs to Him anyway). Then wait for Him, in His time, to direct you in the way He deems best. The point is to allow Him to be in control and not to try to take His rightful place of leadership.

Every ministry or vocation is going to look and function differently. God loves to bless a nearly infinite diversity within His unity. Following God is not a "paint-by-numbers" kit, where you follow a cleverly defined formula for success. It is a process of listening, learning, and patiently following, sometimes in almost complete blindness as you cling to the Almighty hand. Those who want the Christian life to be easy and predictable will find themselves frequently frustrated. God is looking for followers. Jesus didn't give His disciples a ten-year plan. He just woke them every day and said, "Follow Me."

Just as God didn't use the same methods for provision and deliverance with His people in the Bible, so He doesn't use predictable methods with us in our day. The constant is that it is God who leads, God who provides, and God who delivers. The rest is a walk of faith. All I can do in this context is to show you the boxtop, but I can't put all the pieces together for your unique situation.

Your Assignment, Should You Choose to Accept It

When God calls you to a task, He always provides the means for you to be able to accomplish it. Hudson Taylor once said, "The Lord's work, done in the Lord's way will never fail to have the Lord's provision."[2]

Oftentimes, as a leader (whether in the home, church, business, or society), you may feel that you have been left to do something that is beyond your ability. That may be true! You might be in over your head. Perhaps you *can't* raise your children effectively. Perhaps you *can't* disciple the people God has sent your way. Perhaps you *can't* show kindness and compassion to the people you are called to lead. However, *God can*, and He will do His work, His way, *through you*! That is the unique work and call of the Holy Spirit, to empower us to be able to do what we cannot on

2. Neil Girrard, *The Lord's Work and Way*, http://paidionbooks.org/girrard/amlife/workway.html.

our own. Are you willing to let go of whatever is in your hand and surrender it to God and let Him breathe life into it?

Chapter 10

Who Made Your Mouth?

(Evangelism — Moses)

The Lord said to him, "Who has made man's mouth? Or who makes him dumb or deaf, or seeing or blind? Is it not I, the Lord?"

— Exodus 4:11

In recent research polls, analysts were surprised to discover that Americans had two great fears: dying and public speaking. While dying was expected on the list of phobias, very few experts anticipated more participants to report that they were more afraid of speaking than dying!

The thought of giving an address before a group has caused many a brave person to breathe a little harder, get sweaty palms, and experience an increased heart rate. Why is this? Perhaps for some of us, it is a lack of trust in our ability to communicate. We are afraid that our minds will go blank and we will forget what to say. Perhaps we are concerned that our words will come out as a jumbled mess of confusion or contradiction.

As a hyperactive child, my mind worked much quicker than my motor skills. I had so many thoughts that I wanted to express that, when I tried to talk to adults, I couldn't slow down enough to talk clearly. I stuttered and stammered over my words, causing many grown-ups to laugh at my comical attempts to communicate. This, of course, made me frustrated and I would stutter all the more.

Even those who seem confident in public discourse are sometimes privately concerned about how they are perceived by others. The famed Roman orator Marcus Tullius Cicero (106–43 B.C.), was world-renowned in his day (and ours) for his marvelous mastery of Latin prose and orations.

A story is told, however, of someone who saw him privately on the beach one day. He was pacing back and forth speaking to an imaginary audience, with his mouth filled with pebbles! He had determined that learning to speak with his mouth full of rocks would increase his ability to communicate in public.

Feeling Inadequate?

In my life, I have done a lot of public speaking. The Lord helped me to overcome my childhood stuttering issues, and I have been blessed to be able to communicate verbally to tens of thousands.

However, my experiences haven't all been positive. One of my earliest speaking engagements was at a conference in the Midwest. I was one of two speakers at the event with a registered attendance of over 1,000 people. This was pretty big stuff for a young man who was barely out of his teens! I had prepared two messages and was looking forward with much nervous anticipation to speaking to the large audience who would surely come to my sessions.

For weeks beforehand I prepared. Perhaps I over-prepared. I had overheads, bulleted outlines, and compelling illustrations for each major point. When the day of the event arrived, I discovered that this event was housed in two separate buildings. The first was a large gymnasium where dozens of vendors were selling books and materials. The place where I was speaking, on the other hand, was in a building across a hot parking lot (it was July), down two floors in an elevator, through the basement hallway and into a small classroom that seated about 150 people.

You needed a map and a GPS unit to find the place! I was rather crestfallen when I realized that 1,000 people would not be attending my session as I had previously expected.

However, I quickly regained my composure and settled into expecting one-eighth of that figure. When the time came for me to begin my message, there were only 11 people in the room. I was emotionally devastated. I had prepared so hard. I had prayed, seeking the Lord for what He wanted me to share.

Determined to make the best of the situation, I pretended not to be affected by my disappointment and gave my message to the best of my ability. When the session ended, I visited the convention coordinators and asked them if they would please announce my next session over the "loudspeakers" (which consisted of a rented public address system that had an audible range of about 30 feet!), and they assured me that they would.

I comforted myself with the idea that there had been a mix-up with the first session and once the thousand or more attendees heard my next session announced they would fill not only the room, but the hallway and perhaps the elevator as well! Boy, was I going to be disappointed. When my session began there were only seven people in attendance, and two of them were friends of mine who came just to see me!

I can't describe to you how devastated I felt. It was as though God had let me down. I had done my part in preparing the best messages I could, and God was making sport of me by having me talk to empty chairs. As I stepped to the lectern, my feet were like lead. My mouth felt dry, as though I had just won a contest to see who could eat the most peanut butter and crackers before the meeting began.

I breathed deep, said a silent prayer, and decided to give the best presentation to the five people who may have needed to hear my message. I remember vividly two young mothers sitting on the front row to my left. They looked for all the world as though they had made a mistake and stumbled into the wrong room, thinking that someone else was going to be speaking. I felt bad for them. I felt bad for myself. I wanted to tell them, "Look, if you have somewhere else you would rather be, please don't feel obligated to stay."

When I finished my presentation, I dejectedly gathered my notes, overheads, and reference materials and left the lecture hall like a dog with his tail between his legs. To add injury to insult, we sold only 50 dollars worth of books (it cost us much more than that just for gas and hotels to attend), and I inadvertently lost that at a gas station on my way out of town! God and I had a long chat that night on the drive home. For the next few days I stewed and muddled about the event, which had obviously taken a toll on my pride. Finally, I felt the Lord speak to my heart that it was not my job to ensure that lots of people heard my message. It was only my job to present what was on God's heart to the people who came. As Thomas "Stonewall" Jackson once said, "Duty is ours, results belong to God."

Eight years later I was at another conference in the same state. This time I was standing behind our ministry table and a woman walked up to look at our books. When she glanced up at me, she quickly covered her mouth with her hand and then exclaimed, "Stay right there, and don't move, I'm going to get my friend!"

I had no intention of leaving at the moment, but I also had no idea what this woman had in mind. When she excitedly returned with her friend, I immediately recognized these two as the young moms who had, in my mind, "endured" my pitiful presentation years before. They both expressed that that event was a turning point in their lives. I spoke on parenting and the importance of training one's children to the glory of God. That message struck deep in their souls, and they said that the entire trajectory of their families had been altered by what I said that day.

As you can imagine, I was stunned and grateful to God for allowing me to experience the redemption of something that I had written off as a work of futility. You never know how God may use a word or deed to affect another person for eternity.

Who Made Your Mouth?

God once called Moses for the seemingly impossible task of telling Pharaoh to let God's people go. Moses, understandably, didn't jump at the opportunity. Not only would he be unpopular for making such a declaration, he could very well be killed! So Moses did what many of us do. He claimed to be incapable of carrying out God's command.

> Then Moses said to the LORD, "Please, Lord, I have never been eloquent, neither recently nor in time past, nor since You have spoken to Your servant; for I am slow of speech and slow of tongue." The LORD said to him, "Who has made man's mouth? Or who makes him dumb or deaf, or seeing or blind? Is it not I, the LORD? Now then go, and I, even I, will be with your mouth, and teach you what you are to say" (Exod. 4:10–12).

What we must all learn is that the message is not contingent on our abilities. There are only two requirements for sharing the truth of God with others. First, God must be the one who is with us, speaking through us and, secondly, we must be faithful to give His message, without adding our own opinions. God never commands us to do anything without first equipping us.

Little Is Much When God Is in It

Perhaps you are reluctant to share the gospel with a friend, a co-worker, or a neighbor. Maybe you fear that all of your thoughts will come out upside-down and backward. Don't wait for the speaking skills of Billy Graham before you share the life-giving truth of Jesus Christ with someone else. In fact, if a shy, unknown Sunday school teacher named Edward Kimball had been too nervous to share the gospel with a young shoe salesman, we might never even have known the name Billy Graham.

Kimball had felt a leading from the Lord to talk to a young man named Dwight who worked as a clerk at a local shoe store, but like many of us, he was nervous. Finally overcoming his fear of ridicule and rejection, he presented young Dwight with his need for a Savior. Much to his surprise, young Dwight not only accepted Christ, but later became the world-renowned evangelist D.L. Moody.

Years later, Moody was influential in the life of another young man who came to Moody with doubts about his salvation. Moody could have never anticipated that this gangly teenager, who came as a student to a series of meetings at

Lake Forest College in the late 1870s, would someday become (for a brief time) the most influential evangelist in America: J. Wilbur Chapman.

Chapman conducted evangelistic crusades around the nation and trained a young baseball-player-turned-preacher named Billy Sunday. Sunday took what he learned from traveling as Chapman's "set-up man" and became the most famous preacher of the first half of the 20th century.

Sunday, among many other accomplishments, held an evangelistic campaign in Charlotte, North Carolina, in 1924, and a men's prayer and fellowship group, later named the Charlotte Businessmen's Club, grew out of those meetings. This group was later instrumental in inviting Mordecai Ham to Charlotte for a series of evangelistic meetings in 1934.

Billy Graham was an unknown farm lad who was probably considered least likely to become a preacher when he attended those meetings with Ham. In truth, he had gone mainly to ridicule Ham's exuberant speaking style. However, the truth of the gospel cut deep to his heart, and he surrendered his life, and his mouth, to Jesus Christ. Billy Graham has led millions to the Lord, including the man who led Christian leader Charles Colson (founder of Prison Fellowship) to Christ.

Untold millions of souls will be in eternity because of this chain of grace that began with a simple, shy Sunday school teacher. Won't you begin a chain of your own? After all, it isn't about your talent or abilities. It is all about the One who made your mouth.

Chapter 11

Why Are You on Your Face?

(Repentance — Joshua)

The LORD said to Joshua, "Stand up! What are you doing down on your face?"

— Joshua 7:10; NIV

Has life ever felt like you were walking down the road, admiring the beautiful sunshine and glories of creation, and then, all of a sudden, you accidentally fall into an open manhole? It's amazing how quickly circumstances can be altered. Life often transitions with little or no advance warning.

I'm sure that is how Joshua, Moses' successor and the new leader of the Israelites, felt in the story related in Joshua chapter 7. He had just come from one of most astonishing military victories in human history. A rag-tag army of tent-dwelling nomads had just conquered the heavily fortified city of Jericho. Amazingly, the river Jordan was supernaturally parted before them, and the walls of that austere city came down with a trumpet blast and shout.

If there was ever a time to rejoice in the covenant promises of a faithful God, this was it. The whole Israelite camp was pumped up and ready for the next conquest.

The scenario reminds me of times in the past when I have attended revival conferences or special meetings where God's presence is clearly demonstrated and people are being saved or getting right with God. It's an awesome experience.

The hard thing is transitioning back to everyday life after such a spiritual high. At first you feel like you can conquer the world. You are close with God and everything is great. Then you realize that you are still human, and the world, the flesh, and the devil have all conspired to bring you down. There is an enemy lurking in the bushes to devour those who forget to stay close to the Lord.

Sin in the Camp

The presence and blessing of the Lord are directly related to obedience and holiness. If we want to experience the full measure of God's Spirit at work in our lives, we have to allow Him to live fully in and through us.

Yet sometimes the blessing and presence of the Lord seems to grind to a halt and we don't understand why. It may be that we are nurturing a hidden sin that we have not forsaken and abandoned. It may be something we stole from someone through a dishonest business transaction, or unforgiveness toward a family member or former friend, an addiction to pornography or some other self-destructing behavior, or simply pride in ourselves and our own abilities.

These sins may have been accepted and nurtured by us, or our consciences have become so seared that we aren't even aware of the destructive nature of their presence in our lives. We may not realize that they are hindering our fellowship with God and making us vulnerable to devastation and ruin.

Experiencing Defeat

Leaving Jericho, the Israelites spied out the city of Ai and determined that only a few thousand men would be needed to take the city. Given that there were 25,000 people living in Ai, this was perhaps a case of over-confidence, an aftereffect of their previous victory.

Not only were the Israelites routed in their attack on Ai, but they lost 36 lives. Joshua understandably took the loss personally. He tore his clothes and spent the rest of the day face down in the dirt. Joshua's behavior indicated that he was a man who wanted the real presence and blessing of God, not just the mere image.

What Are You Doing?

After a full day of this behavior by Joshua, the Lord met him at night and said to him, "Get up! What are you doing down on your face?" Wow! What a question! I mean, you would expect the Lord to draw him near and speak gently to him, consoling this faithful son for his sincerity and devotion. No such luck.

I know if I was Joshua, I would be thinking, *What do You mean? I'm seeking Your face! I'm humbling myself. I'm trying to find out why we don't have a greater manifestation of Your glory and presence in our midst. I'm weak in the face of worldly opposition. I thought this is what You wanted me to do!*

The Lord gets right to the heart of the matter. "Israel has sinned, and they have transgressed My covenant which I commanded them" (Josh. 7:11). He went on to describe the specific sin of someone stealing plundered items that were to be dedicated to the Lord. "I will not be with you anymore unless you destroy the things under the ban from your midst" (Josh. 7:12).

Hiding in Achan's Tent

We can just forget about moving into the fullness of the things of God until we walk out simple obedience.

The American church is filled with things that God hates: divorce, adultery, fornication, gossip, slander, addictions, lewdness, pride, selfish ambition, and many other forms of immorality. After all of this, we have the audacity to wonder why we do not experience true revival in our day!

Just as the search for Achan, the guilty man, became more and more specific and intense, so the searchlight of the Holy Spirit is probing our hearts. Can we say with King David, "Search me, O God, and know my heart; try me and know my anxious thoughts; and see if there be any hurtful way in me and lead me in the everlasting way" (Ps. 139:23-24)?

It does us no good to spend hours crying out to God for a greater manifestation of His presence if we are not willing to do the simple things He commands. There is no use in praying for greater power or answers to prayer when we are offending the God we claim to serve. Repentance starts with us. Sin isn't merely "out there" somewhere. It is specific and it needs to be dealt with in specific ways. Let's deal with our sins before they not only contaminate our lives, but affect other people as well.

On the positive side, living a holy life opens the door for the flow of God's blessing in our lives. Once the sin is dealt with, we can move forward in victory, conquering the giants in our lives that keep us from possessing all that God has promised to us. There is great joy in living with the assurance that there is nothing standing between us and fellowship with our Creator. It's time to deal with the sin, but then stand up and move forward.

Chapter 12

Who Are These Men with You?

(Syncretism — Balaam)

Then God came to Balaam and said, "Who are these men with you?"

— Numbers 22:9

There is an odd account in the Bible that plays itself out in Number 22–25. It is the story of Balaam, son of Beor. What we remember most about this story from our children's picture Bibles is the fact that God enabled a donkey to speak. I remember as a child being filled with a sense of wonder that at any moment, any one of *my* animals might be enabled by God to speak to me!

As an adult, I think what captures my interest the most is Balaam himself. What kind of a man was he? Was he a good guy or a bad guy? Was he a God-follower or an agent of the devil? Before we explore Balaam, however, let's set up the backdrop for this narrative.

The Israelites have been in the wilderness for many years following the miraculous exodus from Egypt. Moses is old; Miriam and Aaron have both died. The Israelites have increased exponentially, and the inhabitants of Moab and Midian are afraid of them. Both of these people groups are distant relatives of the Israelites. Moab was the son of Lot (Gen. 19:37), born incestuously from his daughter after fleeing Sodom and living in a cave. Midian was a circumcised son of Abraham, whose mother was Keturah (Gen. 25:2).

Both of these men had offspring that chose paths of wickedness. The Moabites worshiped detestable gods named "Chemosh" (1 Kings 11:7), and "Baal-Peor"(Num. 25:1–3), and influenced their Midianite neighbors to do the same. The Midianites, however, retained for many years a knowledge and worship of Yahweh (see Exod. 2:16,

18:9–12). Unlike Moab, whose father had "pitched his tent facing Sodom," the Midianites had righteous Abraham as their father, and their demise into idolatry seems to be slower and more progressive.

Balak, the king of Moab, made an alliance with the Midianites and sought to hire Balaam (whose name means "destruction"), who was famous for his alleged ability to bring blessings or cursings on individuals or even nations. (Note: One of Balaam's non-biblical prophecies has been discovered in an Aramaic text from Deir 'Alla — east of the Jordan River, just north of the Jabbok River.) Through the process of pagan divination, Balak thought that he could seek the favor of the god of the Israelites, and thus gain a military advantage over the Israelites.

At that time, Balaam was living in a city called Pethor (which means, ironically, "Interpretation of Dreams"), near the Euphrates River in northwest Mesopotamia. We don't know Balaam's nationality, but his home was a few miles south of the Hittite capital of Carchemish (the modern-day city is Jerablus in north Syria). To understand the geographic picture, the Israelites are coming from the southwest, heading north into modern-day Israel. Balaam is way, way north of modern-day Israel, in northern Syria, very close to Haran (or Paddan-Aram) where Abraham camped for a while before coming to the Promised Land. Abraham's father is buried there, and Jacob worked for Laban in this region, so it is likely that a godly influence remained in that area. (You really ought to grab a Bible atlas and check out these locations.)

Spiritual Mercenary for Hire

The elders of Moab and Midian made the several-hundred-mile trek to Balaam's house and arrived with a major "donation" to Balaam's ministry in exchange for his participation in cursing the Israelites. They told him they were aware that "whoever you bless is blessed, and whoever you curse is cursed" (Num. 22:6; NIV). Balaam informs the men that they should stay the night and he will see what answer Yahweh gives him. It is interesting to me that although Balaam engages in the practice of divining many gods, he knows which deity he needs to seek for this people group. Is it possible that he was aware of Yahweh's promise to Abraham in Genesis 12:2–3?

> And I will make you a great nation, and I will bless you, and make your name great; and so you shall be a blessing; and I will bless those who bless you, and the one who curses you I will curse. And in you all the families of the earth will be blessed.

When he turned to prayer, God came to him and asked this poignant question: "Who are these men with you?" (Num. 22:9). It seems to me that when God is wanting to get to the heart of the matter, He asks a piercing question that is understood best by the hearer. To me, the pivotal verse to unpacking this mystery is found in Numbers 22:18 where Balaam refers to Yahweh as "my God."

I think that the most sensible reading of this account is to understand Balaam as a man who claimed Yahweh as his primary deity, but made a living of divining any and every god of his day for the sake of building his own wealth and reputation.

Here was a man upon whom the Spirit of God would come (Num. 24:2), who would hear the words of God (vs. 4), and see visions sent from the Almighty (vs. 4). Not only was he operating in the "gifts of the Spirit," he was also fluent in "prophetic ministry." Because of this, he was the most sought-after "keynote speaker" of his day. Balaam was a man who could woo the crowds with his "supernatural revelations." He knew all of the jargon to use. He said all of the right things. "Must I not speak what the LORD puts in my mouth?" (Num. 23:12; NIV). The problem was that his heart was wicked and sinful.

While God restrained him from speaking curses and compelled him to bless the Israelites, Balaam used his cunning knowledge of men's weaknesses to show Balak how to ultimately destroy God's people. His advice was to encourage the Midianite women to seduce the Israelite men into sexual immorality that was mixed with their own pagan idolatry. His plan worked.

Balaams in Our Day

It seems there is a plague of syncretism (the merging of the holy and the profane) in our day within American churches. There are people who parade before television cameras, claiming prophetic knowledge or spiritual gifts, yet they live like the devil and have hearts of greed and envy.

There are "Christian" musicians who sing about Jesus and then broadcast their homosexual lifestyles. There are ministries who compromise the truth to gain more "seed faith" from their donors. There are preachers who teach self-esteem and prosperity, rather than humility and repentance. There are "Christian" publishing houses that promote an "emerging" version of the gospel that denies the authority of Scripture, mocks the importance of holiness, and flaunts a liberal, socialistic agenda cleverly cloaked as a "social gospel."

It isn't metaphorical Moabites and Midianite armies that are the threat; it's the acceptance of worldliness and carnality within the Church. The greatest threat to the Church today is a false gospel that tolerates sin and excuses fleshly behavior.

We need more men and women with the spirit of Joshua. When the Israelites finally possessed the Promised Land and destroyed the pagan inhabitants, Joshua and his men put Balaam to death (Josh. 13:22). Every biblical reference to Balaam after his death is negative.

There are enemies of the Cross, even within the Christian community.

To confront these errors, we don't necessarily need people with Ph.Ds or great credentials. Biblically speaking, any donkey with two eyes and a mouth can do the job. It just takes willingness to do our part. When we see truth being trampled in the streets, we can't remain silent. We must confront the error in a spirit of love and gentleness. We confront the error not because we love exposing error (if this is the case we are surely proud and self-righteous), but rather because we love God and His truth.

The first place we must displace worldliness is in our own hearts. We will be of no help to others if we do not separate ourselves unto the Lord. What if the Lord were to ask us, "Who are these men with you?" What would we say? What alliances have we tolerated in our own lives that displease the Lord? Are we trying to represent Jesus, but still clinging to the images and messages of television, worldly music, and Hollywood? Is there syncretism in our own lives? Do we tolerate a perversion of the truth by embracing the idols of our age in one hand, yet reaching for the true and living God with the other?

Now is the time to repent of our own sins and lovingly speak against the influence of the world and devil in Christ's Church. It is the only way to avoid God's judgment and receive His grace and favor.

Chapter 13

Why Do You Honor Your Sons More than Me?

(Parenting — Eli)

"Why do you honor your sons more than me by fattening yourselves on the choice parts of every offering made by my people Israel?"

— 1 Samuel 2:29; NIV

I once heard a story of a man who felt called by God to be a missionary in a foreign land. Despite the usual dangers involved with such an endeavor, the man felt certain that God desired he and his family take the gospel to a certain area that had never heard about our Lord.

His wife, however, strongly objected when she heard that the land to which they would move was inhabited not only with dangerous natives, but also with deadly, poisonous snakes. Her worries prevailed upon her husband who ultimately felt, despite God's call, that he could not responsibly risk the lives of his sons.

Within a short time, however, his two boys were playing in the backyard of their comfortable American home and were bitten by a rare poisonous snake that inhabited their area. Both boys died from the bites, leaving the grieving parents to mourn not only their loss but to also contemplate the irony of their deaths.

This story, whether legend or genuine, illustrates the point that sometimes people mistakenly honor their children more than the Lord. They don't understand that "In the fear of the LORD is strong confidence: and his children shall have a place of refuge" (Prov. 14:26; KJV). The safest place to be is always in obedience to the Lord.

Honoring Our Children More than the Lord

It has always surprised me that many of the great heroes of the Bible failed so miserably as parents. There are different reasons for their failure, but the net result is always the same.

One of the most important aspects of the Christian life is the process of discipling one's children in the faith. Teaching one's children to know and love God, while foundational and fundamental to Christian orthopraxy, doesn't come natural to many.

The enemy of our souls knows that if he can get your children to rebel against God, he can destroy the godly lineage that is alluded to in Malachi 2:15.

Fathers Who Failed

There is a line of disintegration that begins with Aaron, the first of the Levitical priests, and continues through the lives of the Davidic kings. The curse begins in Leviticus 10 when Aaron's sons, Nadab and Abihu, offer "strange fire" upon the altar of God. The fire of God's holiness emits from His presence and consumes them both instantly. In verse 3 we see that there is nothing their father Aaron can say.

The reason for his silence seems to be hinted at in verse 10 of Leviticus 10. Aaron and his two remaining sons are cautioned on how they can "distinguish between the holy and the common, between the clean and the unclean, and so you can teach the Israelites all the decrees the LORD has given them through Moses" (NIV). Mirroring the pattern of Deuteronomy 6:6–9, Ezra 7:10, and others, the Lord insists that you can only pass on to others what you already possess in your own heart. Aaron was, after all, the man who made the calf of gold and told the people that it was the god who brought them out of Egypt.

Fast-forward to the time of the judges. Eli, a spiritual successor to Aaron, was now the priest who was set apart to lead others into worship of the true God. First Samuel 2:12–17 describes the total disregard that Eli's sons, Hophni and Phinehas, had for the sacredness of their office as priests. They were gluttons, like their father, and took for themselves the choice portions of meat offered in sacrifice. In addition, these two sons fornicated with the women who served at the tent of meeting (vs. 22). Eli attempted to rebuke them, but his words had little effect. Verse 29 reveals that Eli honored his sons more than he honored God. He was living a life that was hypocritical. While saying one thing with his mouth, Eli, through his actions, showed his own disrespect for God's holiness. When both sons died in one day on the battlefield, and the ark of the covenant was taken because of their sin, Eli, being very fat, fell backward off his stool and broke his neck (1 Sam. 4:18).

The young Samuel, raised by Eli, observed all of these events. Samuel was a God-fearing, obedient leader. I always think, *Surely Samuel would take note of Eli's failures and make sure to avoid the same pitfalls once he became a father.* This is not the case. In 1 Samuel 8:1–5, we learn that Samuel appointed his sons as judges for Israel, but his sons did not walk in his ways. They took dishonest bribes and perverted justice, which the Lord hates (see Prov. 12:19). Their reputation was so bad that the people begged Samuel not to depart in death leaving his sons positioned as leaders. They begged for a king.

Samuel anointed the young king David, who as a child doubtless saw Samuel's sons on the covers of the tabloids at the Bethlehem grocery store. David was a man after God's own heart (1 Sam. 13:14). He represented the new kingly order of leadership among the Chosen People. However, he failed to learn the lessons of history regarding fatherhood. He seemed to be very negligent by refusing to address or discipline his sons (see 2 Sam. 13:21, 14:33, and 1 Kings 1:6). The results of his own unbridled lusts and lack of care with his sons is seen in their profligate (albeit short) lives.

His son Solomon wrote most of the Book of Proverbs, including this verse, "The rod and reproof give wisdom: but a child left to himself bringeth his mother to shame" (Prov. 29:15; KJV). Solomon didn't lack wisdom regarding how to raise a child. However, his personal example of sexual indulgence and idolatry drowned out his words of wisdom in the life of his son Rehoboam.

Avoiding Pitfalls

Some parents desire to please their children — to be their friends — so much so that they fail to be good authority figures. Other parents are so distracted by their careers, hobbies, or even ministries that they simply fail to notice or understand what their children are doing. Yet others are very godly people, but they permit other people to direct and train their children's hearts, rather than assuming that responsibility themselves. Furthermore, there are parents who teach their children well, but refuse to live the truth themselves, thereby discrediting their own teaching.

In each of these connected biblical examples, we see men who should have known better. The reason that most of us fail is usually not because we lack information. We usually fail because we don't adequately regard the need for personal holiness and systematic instruction, working hand in hand, as inseparable aspects of our parenting approach. The one without the other will surely fail.

The question before us as Christian parents is, "Who will we honor above all else?" It is only as we honor Christ and put Him first in all things (the Matt. 6:33 principle) that we will be effective in our calling as parents.

Chapter 14

Where Is the House You Will Build for Me?

(Worship — David)

"Where then is a house you could build for Me?"

— Isaiah 66:1

To show their devotion to Allah, strict Muslim believers pray five times daily, facing toward the city of Mecca. Every Friday, the men must say their prayers at noonday inside an Islamic mosque. Finally (among other requirements), at some point in his life he must, if he is able, make a pilgrimage (*Hajj*) to Mecca, which is considered to be a holy city in the Middle East.

Islam has placed a high emphasis on certain locations or sites of ritualistic worship. Islam is not alone, however, in this adherence. Buddhism and Hinduism are both replete with shrines and temples to their prophets or gods.

Luther's Visit to the "House of God"

In 1510, Martin Luther, the Augustinian friar, set out in the cold of winter from Erfurt, Germany, for an approximately 800-mile, month-long hiking trip to Rome. He traveled about through southern Germany, Austria, Liechtenstein, Switzerland, and half of Italy. He walked 26 miles per day to reach the religious shrines and holy places, to do works of penance and gain indulgences.

When Luther finally caught sight of the city of Rome, he fell to his knees and exclaimed, "Holy Rome, I salute thee!" He visited the seven major churches of Rome. Toward the end of his stay, he climbed the *Sancta Scala*, one of the most important sites of the pilgrimage. It was believed that the stairs were the very stairs that Jesus ascended and descended as He stood before Pontius Pilate.

You may wonder how a massive marble staircase was somehow transported 1,428 miles from Jerusalem to Rome.

Good question! In Luther's day, the faithful believed that they had been magically transported by angels. Today it is said that St. Helen, who was Constantine's mother, paid to have them moved.

In an attempt to become closer to God, Luther literally crawled on his hands and knees and kissed each step on his way up. He felt that somehow all of these demonstrations of devotion would gain God's acceptance, and he could finally feel forgiven.

However, after sincerely participating in various religious acts of devotion, Luther still didn't feel any closer to God. Luther left Rome feeling more empty than ever. If God could not be found at the epicenter of church worship in his day, could spiritual connection to God ever be reached?

David's Attempt to Build a House for God

Jerusalem is, in many respects, the center of religious worship throughout the world. It is a center of worship for Jews, Christians, and Muslims. This began during the life of King David, who desired to build a temple, a permanent dwelling place for the name of Yahweh.

In 2 Samuel 7:2, David was bothered by the comparative ease and comfort he had built for his own life and the shabby place he had provided for the Lord. "See now, I dwell in a house of cedar, but the ark of God dwells within tent curtains." David was so zealous to see this endeavor accomplished that he vowed not to allow rest to come to his eyes until the Lord had His rightful dwelling place. It was the *longing* of his heart to build a house for the Lord.

"Surely I will not enter my house, nor lie on my bed; I will not give sleep to my eyes or slumber to my eyelids, until I find a place for the LORD, a dwelling place for the Mighty One of Jacob" (Ps. 132:3–5).

While the Lord was pleased with the heart of the request, things didn't quite work out the way David envisioned. "David found favor in God's sight, and asked that he might find a dwelling place for the God of Jacob. But it was Solomon who built a house for Him. However, the Most High does not dwell in houses made by human hands" (Acts 7:46–48).

The temple Solomon began in 960 B.C. lasted until it was destroyed by Nebuchadnezzar in 586 B.C. (see Jer. 52:13). Zerubbabel began rebuilding another temple 50 years after the previous one had been destroyed, and this smaller one (see Ezra 3:12) lasted until the pompous temple constructed by Herod replaced it beginning in 20 B.C. Herod's towering structure only lasted until A.D. 70 when it was destroyed by the Romans, as Jesus prophesied in Matthew 24:1–2.

During the time of the first temple, the Israelites never stopped going to the temple, but they thought that they could syncretize the worship of Yahweh *and* the pagan gods. Later, the Pharisees worshiped at the temple. They too were very religious, yet the cup was only clean on the outside and filthy on the inside (see Matt. 23). In both cases, the reason the respective temples were destroyed was because the people attended a physical, locational place of worship, but they neglected attendance to the place of worship and honor that God desired to have in their own hearts.

It seems to me that many well-meaning Christians adopt this misguided approach in our day. When I was a (hyperactive) child, I used to run around the church building after meetings chasing my friends and being wild. Inevitably, someone who considered themselves to be the official "sanctuary patrol" would catch me by the arm and admonish me, "Young man, don't you know that you shouldn't run in the *house of God*?" In their homes, many of these people had no problem with swearing at their children, watching worldly movies, or gossiping about the pastor and his wife, but heaven forbid that you should do something inappropriate after entering the doors of "God's house."

Even as a child, I couldn't help but think, *I guess running must never be permissible then, because* my body *is the house of the Lord. Anytime I run, I am running in God's house.*

> Thus says the LORD, "Heaven is My throne, and the earth is My footstool. Where then is a house you could build for Me? And where is a place that I may rest? For My hand made all these things, thus all these things came into being," declares the LORD. "But to this one I will look, to him who is humble and contrite of spirit, and who trembles at My word" (Isa. 66:1–2).

> For thus says the high and exalted One who lives forever, whose name is Holy, "I dwell on a high and holy place, and also with the contrite and lowly of spirit in order to revive the spirit of the lowly and to revive the heart of the contrite" (Isa. 57:15).

While it is true that God's Spirit dwells high in unapproachable light (1 Tim. 6:16), His eyes also search the low places to find those whose hearts are completely His (2 Chron. 16:9).

When Jesus, who was greater than the temple (Matt. 12:6), died, the veil in the temple that divided the Holy Place from the Most Holy Place was torn in two from top to bottom (Matt. 27:51), giving us a new hope for access to God: "And I heard a loud voice from the throne, saying, 'Behold, the tabernacle of God is among men, and He will dwell among them, and they shall be His people, and God Himself shall be among them' " (Rev. 21:3).

After Pentecost, the Holy Spirit indwells not buildings, but *human* temples. "For we are the temple of the living God; just as God said, 'I will dwell in them and walk among them; and I will be their God, and they shall be My people' " (2 Cor. 6:16; see also 1 Cor. 3:16–17, 6:19; Eph. 2:21.)

If only we could be as zealous for the true dwelling of God (involving a humble and contrite heart within us) as some people are for their religious buildings and structures. Oh, that we would be like David and give ourselves no rest until we have made a place of honor for the Lord in our hearts (the spiritual Jerusalem).

> On your walls, O Jerusalem, I have appointed watchmen; all day and all night they will never keep silent. You who remind the Lord, take no rest for yourselves; and give Him no rest until He establishes and makes Jerusalem a praise in the earth (Is. 62:6–7).

Chapter 15

What Are You Doing Here?

(Purpose — Elijah)

"What are you doing here, Elijah?"

— 1 Kings 19:13

The late Larry Burkett, who advised many people regarding their finances and career decisions, told a story about a medical doctor who made a good income, yet squandered it all year after year in the pursuit of "get-rich-quick" schemes. After spending some time counseling with Burkett, the man understood that his pursuit of instant wealth was based on a desire to make enough money to retire early from the medical field. You see, his father had been a medical doctor, and so, by default, he chose the path of least resistance and entered a career that he hated. After coming to grips with his true motivations, he left the medical profession and became a construction worker, something he felt the Lord wanted him to do.

I'm sure there are a lot of construction workers who would shake their heads and say, why would someone give up a lucrative salary in the medical field to take on the laborious task of building? The answer is calling. Each life is unique and has a special destiny. When you aren't fulfilling your destiny, you feel lost and out of place with the world around you.

Many of the most popular current bestsellers have brought attention to one of the biggest problems in the Church today: people are not fulfilling their destiny. I recently heard a popular Christian speaker deliver a message to a Christian audience (including many church leaders). He asked them to raise their hands if they *knew* that they were not fulfilling God's call on their lives. Two-thirds of the audience responded! Now, if he had said, "How many of you aren't sure whether or not you are fulfilling

God's purpose for your life?" or something nebulous like that, I wouldn't have been surprised, but to see that many Christians admit that they knew they were out of step with God's will was distressing to say the least.

Hiding Out

In 1 Kings 19, we read an amazing account of the prophet Elijah who was just coming down from the most incredible spiritual high of his prophetic career. In the previous chapter, he encountered the false prophets of Baal on Mount Carmel and called fire from heaven to consume his sacrifice. After slaying the bad guys, the zeal of the Lord came upon him and he ran ahead of Ahab's chariot approximately 16 miles from Carmel to Jezreel. This guy was on top of the world! However, in the first two verses of chapter 19, he receives a death threat from perhaps the most infamous woman in history, Queen Jezebel. Elijah was terrified and ran again, this time for his life!

He ends up in Beersheba, which was the southernmost tip of the kingdom, leaves his servant there, and travels a day's journey by himself into the desert (beyond the scope of known civilization). Exhausted, he collapses on the ground and says, "I've had enough, Lord. Take my life." Have you ever had a day like that?

An angel meets him, gives him nourishment, and Elijah gets up and continues his travels. For 40 days and nights, he travels through the desert until he reaches Mount Horeb (Mount Sinai), the mountain of God. If you look at a map and consider his reaction (Mount Horeb is about 250 miles from Beersheeba), this man was having a serious panic attack! Going to Mount Horeb would be like you booking it to the North Pole! As if that isn't enough, he finds a cave and crawls in it.

Personally, I appreciate the truthful disclosure of the Bible as it reveals the humanity of the heroes of the faith. They were imperfect, just as we are (see James 5:17 concerning Elijah).

Confronted by God

At this point, God enters the scene. "What are you doing here, Elijah?" I love this. God is so awesome in His understanding of human nature. Of course, God isn't scratching His head wondering, "What has gotten into this boy?" No, he is trying to get Elijah to open up and be honest about his own feelings and struggles. Elijah says (my paraphrase), "Look, I've been a faithful prophet. I've been operating in my calling while all the other Israelites have bailed out. They have broken Your covenant, torn down Your altars, and they try to kill people who have the word 'Prophet' on their business card. Now I am the only one left, and they are trying to kill me too!"

There is a lot that could be said here. Over 550 years before, Moses, who represented the Law (God's covenant), was sustained by God on this same mountain for 40 days and 40 nights. Not only was Elijah trying to place as much distance as he could between himself and Jezebel, but I believe he was in a personal struggle to find the very roots or foundations of his faith. It seemed to him that everything that God had promised under the Mosaic era had come to nothing. He was now in the position of representing, more than any other man, the new era of God's prophetic ministry, and he wanted to see if the same God who met Moses in such a personal and powerful way would meet with *him*. Yes, he had seen God's power on Mount Carmel (representing the pinnacle of his public ministry), but that was different. Elijah's visit to Mount Horeb was a silent request to see if God would show up in the total isolation of his private world.

> And [God] said, Go forth, and stand upon the mount before the LORD. And, behold, the LORD passed by, and a great and strong wind rent the mountains, and brake in pieces the rocks before the LORD; but the LORD was not in the wind: and after the wind an earthquake; but the LORD was not in the earthquake: and after the earthquake a fire; but the LORD was not in the fire: and after the fire a still small voice (1 Kings 19:11–12; KJV).

What Are You Listening To?

Wind, earth, and fire represent the elements of this world. You can't base direction for your life on what you see raging around you. You can't gauge your calling or destiny on the chaos of your circumstance. You can't make a career change based on the difficulty of the work or even a death threat. You have to keep listening for the only sure and trustworthy guide in the universe . . . the still small voice of God.

Again, God repeats His question: "What are you doing here, Elijah?" Elijah gives the same impassioned answer. God responds by saying, "Go back the way you came." God wasn't done with Elijah. He had more work for him to do. In fact, He was just beginning to set in motion the mechanism that would destroy the kingdom of Ahab and provide a successor for Elijah, to carry on the work after his "retirement" into eternity. Good things were just around the bend. God informs Elijah that, despite Elijah's gloomy feeling of loneliness, there are seven thousand, reserved to Himself, who have not bowed their knees to Baal or kissed him.

As a side note, neither Elijah nor Moses saw the completion of the promise in their lifetime. However, on a different mountain many years later (the Mount of Transfiguration), they were able to see the embodiment of God's covenant promise being fulfilled in the person of Jesus Christ.

Why Don't We Live Our Destiny?

There are several reasons that we don't fulfill the purpose for which God has created us.

We Don't Seek God

The first is that we don't seek God to understand His will. "If any of you lack wisdom, let him ask of God, that giveth to all men liberally, and upbraideth not; and it shall be given him" (James 1:5; KJV; see also Prov. 3:5–7, 16:9, 20:24 and Jer. 10:23). If the Lord knows all the days of our lives before we are even born (Ps. 139:16), we surely cannot presume that He will bless any old direction we wish to head in life. He has a specific plan for us (see Jer. 29:11; Rom. 12:1; and 1 Cor. 6:20).

Fear (Unbelief)

Secondly, we often refuse to move into our calling because of fear. It may be fear of man, fear of failure, fear of the unknown, or some other apprehension.

Fear of Man — For Elijah, it was fear of man (or woman as the case may be), which Proverbs 29:25 says will bring a snare.

Fear of Failure — Fear of failure has kept many people from moving forward into the promises of God. We don't want to go out on a limb and look bad to our friends if things don't pan out the way we hoped they would. This is reasonable if we are simply acting on our own wishes or desires. However, when God has given a command or a promise, He is faithful to complete it (Phil. 1:6; Isa. 55:11). We need to remember that we don't accomplish the work by our strength or willpower, but by God's spirit working in and through us (Zech. 4:6–7; Eph. 6:12).

Fear of the Unknown — I have often observed people who hate their current status in life, but refuse to move forward into something new because the misery of their current situation feels safer to them than what may be lurking around the bend. Moses and Gideon come to mind as examples of men who really didn't want to leave the safety of obscurity to do great things for God. God told Gideon, "Go in this thy might, and thou shalt save Israel from the hand of the Midianites: *have not I sent thee?*" (Judg. 6:14; KJV; emphasis mine).

Discouragement

Elijah allowed himself to be ruled by an earthly perspective of what he saw around him. We can fall into the same trap if we aren't vigilant. We must not allow ourselves to be defined by our environment or circumstance. If we are focused on ourselves, our propensities, our past, or our feelings, we will fail to press into the promised blessings that lie ahead.

Living by Default, Not Design

There is a laziness or passivity that often keeps us from pressing into the Promised Land. We are content with the shabby conditions of our lives and the world around us. We are lured into believing that our present circumstance is tolerable and therefore isn't worth the effort to improve. We need to remember that we aren't the masters of our own destiny. Life isn't about what we want. We are servants of the Most High God, and we must report for duty. We must discover what tasks the Master has for us. We can't merely bury the talent the Lord has given us because we have adopted a mindset of defeat.

The story of Elijah reminds us that we need to continue to seek the face of God in both the high times and the low.

We need to trust in His sovereign hand to lead and guide us. We need to press into the calling we have received until the day that the Lord sends His fiery chariots to take us home to our reward. Until that day comes, we can't abandon the battle. We don't want to be found by the Lord in the wrong place, at the wrong time, doing the wrong things. So take some time and examine your heart. What are you doing here? Are you where the Lord wants you to be?

Chapter 16

Who Should We Send? Who Will Go for Us?

(Missions — Isaiah)

"Whom shall I send, and who will go for Us?"

— Isaiah 6:8

There is an old adage in the military that says, "Don't be the first, don't be the last, keep your mouth shut and never volunteer for anything!" The idea is that you don't want to stand out or you will get stuck with really lousy jobs that nobody wants to do.

While there may be some earthly wisdom in that advice given over the years to young conscripted soldiers, in the Kingdom of God there is a great need for volunteers.

A Loss of Reverence

The year was 740 b.c. and King Uzziah had just died. Uzziah (also called Azariah) was appointed by the people to be king at the age of 16 (2 Kings 14:21; 2 Chron. 26:1). He ruled for 52 years and oversaw a great reconstruction period for the people of Judah.

In his younger years, under the guidance of the prophet Zechariah, he was faithful to God, and "did right in the sight of the LORD" (2 Kings 15:3; 2 Chron. 26:4). However, as he entered old age, he became confident in himself, and entered the temple of the Lord to burn incense on the altar (2 Chron. 26:15–16), which was forbidden for anyone but the priests. The Lord struck him with leprosy, and until the day he died, he had to live in isolation (2 Kings 15:5).

Not only did Uzziah experience separation in his final days, but he was not "buried with his fathers," which was the great honor of the Hebrew culture. He was instead buried in an adjacent field.

This must have had a devastating effect on the people of Israel. The closest thing we can relate it to politically would probably be the impeachment of Richard Nixon in America in the 1970s. Great shock and sadness would have engulfed the people.

A Vision of the Lord

It is in this historical context that the prophet Isaiah has a powerful encounter with Almighty God. In contrast to the irreverent display of Uzziah's contempt for the Lord's temple, Isaiah sees the Lord "high and lifted up," with His glory filling the temple. The seraphs (angels) were flying and declaring to one another, "Holy, holy, holy is the LORD of hosts, the whole earth is full of His glory" (Isa. 6:1–3; KJV).

The revelation of God to Isaiah is primarily focused on His holiness. In the Hebrew language, there is no punctuation, so if you want to add an exclamation point to emphasize something, you say it twice. God does this when He meets Moses at the burning bush. "Moses, Moses!" This should stop you in your tracks and make you pay attention. This is a vital, imperative notification!

Furthermore, in the Hebrew language, if you wish to say something with as much force and magnification as possible, the greatest superlative is to repeat it three times. The seraphs declare that God is holy. But He is not merely holy with an exclamation point! God is *infinitely* holy! He is more holy than it is possible to be holy. God is *that* kind of holy.

This God will not be trifled and dismissed by the low view His people have of Him. He will not stand by idly and allow His holy presence to be desecrated by king or peasant.

The Fear of the Lord

This revelation of God as infinitely holy is at the same time both frightening and comforting. It means that God, as a just judge, will not wink at sin and disobedience. But it also means that He is still alive and dedicated to maintaining His covenant with His people. He hasn't abandoned His followers or left them to their own devices. God Himself will be their hope and strength as they move forward into the unknown future.

The very doorposts and thresholds of the temple shake, and the temple is filled with smoke in response to the angels' worship. Isaiah, watching this spectacular display, exclaims, "Woe is me, for I am ruined! Because I am a man of unclean lips, and I live among a people of unclean lips; for my eyes have seen the King, the LORD of hosts" (Isa. 6:5).

A seraph flew over to Isaiah with a burning coal held in tongs from the incense altar. He touched the lips of Isaiah and declared him cleansed and forgiven. This is a symbol of what God has done for each of us, through Christ. We can stand before the presence of this infinitely holy God as righteous, not because of ourselves, but because of Christ's atonement.

The Commission

Then the Lord speaks and says, "Whom shall I send, and who will go for Us?" (Isa. 6:8). It is interesting to consider to whom this question is addressed. Was it to the seraphs? God uses both the singular and the plural pronouns here. Is He conversing within Himself (within the Godhead)? Is He saying this for Isaiah's benefit, hoping for a volunteer?

Whatever the case, the response to this call on the part of Isaiah is immediate.

When you see the Lord as He truly is, then you see yourself as you really are. Typically, we have a very over-inflated view of ourselves. Too often we tend to think that we are awesome, and other people are failures and misfits. When we experience a relational conflict, we naturally assume that the other person is entirely to blame, and we are mere victims who are misunderstood and falsely judged.

All of that goes by the wayside when we encounter the presence of the living God. We see ourselves, in our flesh, as wretchedly sinful and beyond any hope (apart from Christ's redemption). We also see ourselves in context with others. We are sinful people, living amongst sinful people. Finally, when we see God as He really is, and ourselves as we truly are, we are enabled to see others the way God sees them. He sees them with love and mercy and compassion.

> The Lord is . . . patient toward you, not wishing for any to perish but for all to come to repentance (2 Pet. 3:9).

Will You Go?

There are over seven billion people on the planet, and over five billion of them make no claim of following Christ at all. This generation of Christians is responsible for the evangelism of this generation of souls. Have you had an encounter with the living God? Have you seen the depths of your own need and your own inadequacy apart from Christ? Do you have a love for other people and a desire to reach them with the love and truth of Christ? Are you willing to raise your hand, speak up, and volunteer for the Lord's service?

> Do you not say, "There are yet four months, and then comes the harvest"? Behold, I say to you, lift up your eyes and look on the fields, that they are white for harvest. Already he who reaps is receiving wages and is gathering fruit for life eternal; so that he who sows and he who reaps may rejoice together (John 4:35–36).

The time is now! Are you willing to be a laborer in the harvest?

Chapter 17

Do You Have a Right to be Angry?

(Sovereignty — Jonah)

The Lord said, "Do you have good reason to be angry?"

— Jonah 4:4

Have you ever noticed that many atheists are awfully angry at a God in whom they don't believe? They say they don't believe in His existence, but whenever something bad happens in their life or some national tragedy occurs, they begin to rail at this deity and question His goodness and benevolence.

It's interesting how we humans often want it both ways. We want a God who is big enough to solve all of our problems and keep us out of any kind of danger or illness, but we want one small enough to submit to our demands and do things the way we want them done.

The problem with this dilemma is the issue of sovereignty. By definition, whoever is the Supreme Ruler of the universe gets to call the shots. He gets to be in control, not us.

The Runaway Prophet

Jonah, son of Amittai (meaning "Truth"), appears in 2 Kings as a prophet from Gath-hepher (a few miles north of Nazareth). He was active in ministry during the reign of Jeroboam II (c.786–746 B.C.).

He was called to go preach against the city of Nineveh. It was a vast city, with 120,000 people (Jon. 4:11). It took three days to walk from one end to the other (Jon. 3:3).

In Genesis 10:11, in the King James Version, we are told that Asshur originally built the city of Nineveh, shortly after the Flood of Noah's day, around the time of the construction of the Tower of Babel. Other Bible translations attribute this to Nimrod. Ashur later appears as the chief deity of the Assyrians. The location of the ancient city of Nineveh is near modern-day Mosul in Iraq.

The Assyrians were a ruthless and bloodthirsty people. Their *Assyrian War Bulletin* from about 1000 B.C. tells of them impaling prisoners on stakes, flaying nobles, spreading their skins out on piles, burning them on fires, and cutting off limbs, noses, ears, and fingers. They would often put out the eyes of their prisoners or make pyramids of their heads. You can understand why Jonah might not want to go hang out with these people. So Jonah went to Joppa, hopped a boat, and headed to Tarshish (which was on the farthest end of the known world . . . in the opposite direction!).

Was Jonah a Real Person?

While many secular historians and scientists (and even a few theologians) have been skeptical about the existence of Jonah, our Lord referenced his life and the account of his being swallowed by a large fish as being accurate.

> But He answered and said to them, "An evil and adulterous generation craves for a sign; and yet no sign will be given to it but the sign of Jonah the prophet; for just as Jonah was three days and three nights in the belly of the sea monster, so will the Son of Man be three days and three nights in the heart of the earth. The men of Nineveh will stand up with this generation at the judgment, and will condemn it because they repented at the preaching

of Jonah; and behold, something greater than Jonah is here" (Matt. 12:39–41; see also Luke 11:29–32).

A Proclamation of Judgment

You know the story about how Jonah and the men on the boat met a storm, he was thrown overboard, swallowed by a large fish, and three days later regurgitated onto dry land. He got up, headed into Nineveh, and preached against it. Ironically, he doesn't tell the people to repent. He only says, "Yet forty days and Nineveh will be overthrown" (Jon. 3:4).

Much to his chagrin, however, the people repent! Worse yet, God relents and doesn't send judgment. This is a bad day in Jonah's world. You see, Jonah doesn't like these people. When the question is asked, "Why do bad things happen to good people?" it is usually the Assyrians who are doing the bad things to the good people!

> But it greatly displeased Jonah and he became angry. He prayed to the LORD and said, "Please LORD, was not this what I said while I was still in my own country? Therefore in order to forestall this I fled to Tarshish, for I knew that You are a gracious and compassionate God, slow to anger and abundant in lovingkindness, and one who relents concerning calamity. Therefore now, O LORD, please take my life from me, for death is better to me than life." The LORD said, "Do you have good reason to be angry?" (Jon. 4:1–4).

Jonah went out to the east side of the city, set up a little shelter, and sat down to see what would happen to the city. He was going to wait out the 40 days, just in case the fire from heaven fell after all.

So the Lord caused a leafy plant to grow up and cover Jonah to give him shade from the sun. Jonah liked this plant, and its shade very much. In one of the more benign arguments in Church history, Jerome and Augustine disagreed on whether this was a gourd (Augustine) or a kind of ivy (Jerome). Technically, Jerome thought it was neither, but he thought ivy was closer. These are, of course, the things that split churches and cause the rise of new denominations!

Whatever the nature of the plant, it was useful to Jonah for a very practical reason. After three days being partially digested inside of a great fish, it is very probable that Jonah's skin would have been altered and become very sensitive to the sun.

The very next day, God caused a worm to eat the plant and it withered. Then God brought a scorching east wind and the hot sun to beat down on Jonah. Needless to say, Jonah wasn't happy. Jonah "became faint and begged with all his soul to die, saying, 'Death is better to me than life' " (Jon. 4:8).

Do You Have a Right to be Angry?

Then God said to Jonah, "Do you have good reason to be angry about the plant?" And he said, "I have good reason to be angry, even to death." (Jon. 4:9).

Why did God ask this question? What does God want Jonah to consider about himself, his situation, and the people of Nineveh?

Let's consider for a moment the last hotel where Jonah stayed. It was dark, damp, and smelled like rotten fish. From that underwater tomb, Jonah cried out to God for mercy. He had no justification that he could offer. He was guilty of rebellion against God. He was without hope or excuse. Who does that sound like? The Ninevites, perhaps?

> Then the LORD said, "You had compassion on the plant for which you did not work and which you did not cause to grow, which came up overnight and perished overnight. Should I not have compassion on Nineveh, the great city in which there are more than 120,000 persons who do not know the difference between their right and left hand, as well as many animals?" (Jon. 4:10–11).

The book suddenly ends with no real resolution. I believe one reason for that may be that God wants to leave the question with us, the readers. Do we have a right to be angry about the decisions God makes? Do we have a right to question His authority? Who is the sovereign king of the universe — us or God? We have been shown *so much* mercy. How can we not be willing to extend it to others? How can we not trust God, knowing that what He allows, or sends, is always best?

Chapter 18

Is My Hand Too Short?

(Omnipotence — Hezekiah)

"Is My hand so short that it cannot ransom? Or have I no power to deliver?"

— Isaiah 50:2

Have you ever proclaimed that you are trusting God, only to discover that you aren't *really* trusting Him at all? I tend to do that . . . a lot. I often think I'm trusting God as long as I know that a situation is well within my own natural ability to manage and control. For some reason, I tend to function as though God is only able to do what I can do.

In about 700 B.C., King Hezekiah of Judah was faced with an invasion by the wicked Assyrian tyrant Sennacherib. Judah had already been plundered and was in no position to defend itself. After receiving very descriptive threats about what would happen to them, Hezekiah threw himself on the mercy of Yahweh.

The prophet Isaiah came to the king, promising him that the Lord had indeed heard his prayers and was poised to rescue them. Hezekiah needed to know that God was in control. God's message to Hezekiah was in question form: "Is My hand so short that it cannot ransom? Or have I no power to deliver?" (Isaiah 50:2).

The question at hand is, "Who is in control?" If it was left up to Hezekiah and his soldiers, there was absolutely no hope. They weren't strong enough to pull off a victory. On the other hand, the Creator of heaven and earth certainly was!

That night, the angel of the Lord went through the enemy camp and when dawn broke, 185,000 Assyrians lay dead. The battle was over before it began (see 2 Kings 18:13–19:36).

God Can Do His Sovereign Will

> "Ah Lord God! Behold, You have made the heavens and the earth by Your great power and by Your outstretched arm! Nothing is too difficult for You" (Jer. 32:17).

Over 150 years before the threat by Sennacherib, the prophet Elisha's life was threatened by Ben-Haddad II. He was upset that his military schemes were constantly thwarted because Elisha informed the king of Israel of his every move. How did Elisha know? So he sent his army to surround the city where Elisha was staying.

Talk about a bad start to your day! Imagine waking up, looking out the window, and seeing hundreds of horses and chariots and perhaps thousands of foot soldiers. "What do they want?" you ask a friend.

"Oh, not much. They say if we hand you over, nobody will get hurt." Elisha's servant was understandably concerned. Elisha, however, wasn't the slightest bit disturbed.

> So he answered, "Do not fear, for those who are with us are more than those who are with them." Then Elisha prayed and said, "O Lord, I pray, open his eyes that he may see." And the Lord opened the servant's eyes and he saw; and behold, the mountain was full of horses and chariots of fire all around Elisha (2 Kings 6:16–17).

The question at hand is *not* the strength of the Lord. He is almighty over all. The voice that spoke the universe into

135

existence can handle any struggle or difficulty we might face.

Receiving His Protection

God is ready and willing to come to our defense when we call on His name. Sometimes, however, we make ourselves vulnerable by removing ourselves from under God's protective covering.

> Behold, the LORD's hand is not so short that it cannot save; nor is His ear so dull that it cannot hear. But your iniquities have made a separation between you and your God, and your sins have hidden His face from you, so that He does not hear (Isa. 59:1–2).

Just like sheep, we need to stay close to the shepherd. We are so helpless on our own. We are so inept and unable to provide for our own needs. We need to humble ourselves, acknowledging that we are not God and that if He does not intervene on our behalf, we have no hope.

> "For My hand made all these things, thus all these things came into being," declares the LORD. "But to this one I will look, to him who is humble and contrite of spirit, and who trembles at My word" (Isa. 66:2).

Humbling ourselves under the mighty hand of God releases the power of God to work on our behalf. If we are under proper submission to Him, we know that in due time, He will lift us up (see 1 Pet. 5:6).

Consider the situations in which you find yourself today. Do you feel overwhelmed? Does it seem that the circumstances in your life are greater than your ability to control them? Do you feel hopeless and helpless? Who is in charge? Do you really trust that God knows what is best, and that nothing can happen to you that He does not allow (for your good and His glory!)? Are you willing to let go of your fears and embrace faith? God's hand is *not* too short. He is mighty to save!

Chapter 19

Constant Change
(Sanctification)

"Has He said, and will He not do it? Or has He spoken, and will He not make it good?"

— Numbers 23:19

My one-and-a-half-year-old daughter recently achieved a deeper level of "self-awareness." No, she hasn't been watching Shirley MacLaine or practicing her yoga techniques. This radical entry into greater realms of "conscious self-knowingness" will doubtless serve as an axis on which much of her future life will pivot.

With a furrowed brow and a wrinkled nose, she recently tugged on her mother's skirt, pointed repeatedly toward her diaper, and uttered a word which neither her mother, nor I, had ever systematically taught her. With pleading and desperate eyes she begged, "Change!"

My wife and I also had a moment of illumination as it dawned on us in a new and enlightened way that our daughter was more in tune with life than we had previously thought. "Admitting that you have a problem is the first step to getting help," declared my wife as she doled out sympathetic and therapeutic consolations to our newly aware daughter. And within minutes, "Mama's Quick Lube," home of the two-minute diaper change, had taken care of the problem.

The Philosophy of Change

This desire for change in the life of my daughter has recalled to my mind one of the great oxymorons in our human experience: *the constancy of change.* In pre-Socratic philosophy, the 6th-century thinker Heraclitus made the following statement: "The only thing that is permanent in the universe is change." He made the claim that you cannot step into the same river twice. If you put your left foot in the river, by the time you take it out (and shake it all about), the river has performed the *hocus-pocus* and moved on. So the river you place your right foot in, is not, technically speaking, the same river.

The Certainty of Change

It seems the only thing we can be certain of in this life is that life will change. I know of a family that relocated 21 times in 20 years. There is no certainty in the economy, our employment status, or our health. It appears that only change is inevitable.

The Changeless One

The nature of God, on the other hand, is quite different from the earth in which we live. He is constant and immutable.

In Numbers 29, God said: "God is not a man, that He should lie, nor a son of man, that He should repent; has He said, and will He not do it? Or has He spoken, and will He not make it good?" (Num. 23:19).

God's dealings with people may vary in time/space history, but He is unmoved by any force outside of Himself. There is nothing more powerful than God. James 1:17 declares that with our Father, there is neither variableness, nor shadow of turning. How unlike us. God never changes, because He doesn't need to. He is perfect and entire, lacking nothing. This should be our goal also (see James 1:4).

A Culture of Change

The dilemma of change is endemic to our postmodern pop culture. Ken Myers, an author and cultural analyst, once told me in an interview that pop culture is based on a principle of "planned obsolescence." In other words, consumerism is built on the concept that we should never be satisfied with what we have. We always need bigger, faster, better, more expensive, and more, well . . . hip.

The Paradox of Change

In the realm of theology, however, we find the antithesis of this notion. When we study the Scriptures, we find an interesting paradox. We are taught that we should be content, yet still desire change. This is not, of course, a contradiction. In logic, the law of non-contradiction states that "Two opposing statements cannot both be true at the same time and *in the same way.*" The reason this is a paradox (a true statement that appears to be false or contradictory) is because the Bible is referring to two different issues.

Material Needs

First of all, in terms of material things (the stuff of earth), we are told repeatedly to be content with what we have. We should stop desiring and demanding more. In Philippians 4:11–13, the Apostle Paul says, in regard to wealth, "I have learned, in whatsoever state I am, therewith to be content. I know both how to be abased, and I know how to abound: everywhere and in all things I am instructed both to be full and to be hungry, both to abound and to suffer need. I can do all things through Christ which strengtheneth me" (KJV).

Spiritual Needs

Yet, this same writer a chapter earlier admonishes us in regard to spiritual maturity, "Not as though I had already attained, either were already perfect: but I follow after, if that I may apprehend that for which also I am apprehended of Christ Jesus. Brethren, I count not myself to have apprehended: but this one thing I do, forgetting those things which are behind, and reaching forth unto those things which are before, I press toward the mark for the prize of the high calling of God in Christ Jesus" (Phil. 3:12–14; KJV).

Isn't this the opposite of how we often live? We are so content with our spiritual life. We think we are doing pretty well overall. We live morally above our neighbors, we go to church, and we don't cheat old ladies out of their life savings. We tend to rest on our haunches, pat ourselves on the back, and stay the same as we have been. We resist spiritual growth and maturity, which requires change.

Seeing Our Need for Change

In regard to material wealth, however, we act like starved maniacs, champing at the bit for a slightly larger slice of the proverbial pie. We are ravenous in our pursuit of "just a little bit more." What a stench this must leave in our Savior's nostrils.

> So because you are lukewarm, and neither hot nor cold, I will spit you out of My mouth. Because

you say, "I am rich, and have become wealthy, and have need of nothing," and you do not know that you are wretched and miserable and poor and blind and naked, I advise you to buy from Me gold refined by fire so that you may become rich, and white garments so that you may clothe yourself, and that the shame of your nakedness will not be revealed; and eye salve to anoint your eyes so that you may see. Those whom I love, I reprove and discipline; therefore be zealous and repent (Rev. 3:16–19).

If only we ourselves could see as God does, we would realize how we are wallowing in the filthy lucre of this world. Our obsession with more and our willingness to wallow in spiritual complacency have left us in a truly miserable condition. If only we could grasp how much better it feels to be clean; to be willing to be changed, so that we can grow to maturity as spiritual adults, and not be dwarfed, spiritual infants our whole lives. We need the eye salve of the Holy Spirit to illumine to us how nice it is to have the filth of the world removed from our lives. May we, with childlike simplicity and trust, furrow our brow, wrinkle our nose, and plead to our Heavenly Father, "Change!"